Giving Together

Also available by Carol A. Wehrheim
from Westminster John Knox Press

Getting It Together: Spiritual Practices for Faith, Family, and Work

Giving Together

A Stewardship Guide for Families

Carol A. Wehrheim

Westminster John Knox Press
LOUISVILLE • LONDON

Scripture quotations from the New Revised Standard Version of the Bible are copyright © 1989 by the Division of Christian Education of the National Council of the Churches of Christ in the U.S.A. and are used by permission.

Cover illustration and design by RohaniDesign.com

First edition
Published by Westminster John Knox Press
Louisville, Kentucky

This book is printed on acid-free paper that meets the American National Standards Institute Z39.48 standard. ∞

PRINTED IN THE UNITED STATES OF AMERICA

04 05 06 07 08 09 10 11 12 13 — 10 9 8 7 6 5 4 3 2 1

Library of Congress Cataloging-in-Publication Data

Wehrheim, Carol A.
    Giving together : a stewardship guide for families / by Carol A. Wehrheim.— 1st ed.
        p. cm.
    Includes bibliographical references.
    ISBN 0-664-22689-2 (alk. paper)
    1. Family—Religious life. 2. Stewardship, Christian. I. Title.

BV4526.3.W445 2004
248'.6—dc22

                                                                            2003055563

Contents

Giving Together

Introduction

Go to a large bookstore and you will find shelf upon shelf of books about saving money, spending money, making money, and living within your means, not to mention books about traveling on a few dollars a day and decorating on a shoestring. On other shelves are cookbooks for low-cost, high-nutrition meals and volumes on repairing your own car or building your own house.

Not only are these books available, but additional publications and magazine articles warn parents about the need to teach their children to be smart consumers and money-wise participants in today's economy. In research for a presentation on preteens, the greatest number of—and most disturbing—articles were found in the business sections of major newspapers: articles on this age group as consumers.

Turn to most books on the church and stewardship, and they will tell you how to run a successful stewardship campaign or build the financial giving of your congregation. You might expect a book about families and stewardship to be just another book lined up on those shelves. However, two things set this book apart: 1. few of those books include any word about giving or philanthropy, and 2. this book explores a broader definition of stewardship, because how we spend our money is just one piece of the stewardship pie chart.

More than Money

While money and finances often come to mind first when church members hear the word *stewardship*, Christian stewardship is about the choices we make, choices that reveal the role of faith in one's life. The choices we make—the vacation we plan or the music we listen to—are about how we understand God's world and our place in it. These choices also affect how we relate to other family members and how we interact with people outside the family. Stewardship is how lives are lived in God's world and how we use our gifts from God. In families, we make these stewardship choices individually as well as together, and all those decisions affect family life.

Even as a family makes decisions about the use of its financial resources, other areas of life together beg for attention as well. Today, the amount of time the family has to spend together is also a stewardship issue. The way that time is "spent" is critical when families can barely come together for one meal once a week because the schedules of family members make that impossible. An important role of any family is passing on its heritage and the Christian faith. This requires time together and a concerted effort to establish the rit-

uals that will accomplish the task. Many families today need first to ponder their stewardship of time, setting it alongside their mission as a family unit in the body of Christ.

The Christian family must also examine how it uses its gifts or talents, corporately and individually, to support the mission of its congregation. When one family member chooses to join a committee or sing in the choir, the time and energy required to meet this commitment is not available to the family. The family can discuss the consequences of one member's call and how it will affect the way the necessary tasks of daily life are allotted. This too is a stewardship task of the family.

The Christian calling is not confined to matters within the congregation, however. As children join scout troops or participate in after-school activities, the stewardship of the family toward the community must be altered. We are called to care for our neighbors as well, serving them out of our generosity. Pondering this part of the stewardship picture leads families to examine what money to contribute, as well as to whom to contribute it.

Along with the community as a setting for stewardship, the stewardship of the environment cannot be overlooked. As caretakers of this planet, each family member must ponder how to use natural resources. Specific choices and actions about preserving this earth are before families daily.

The final chapter helps you look at advocacy for others as a way of seeking justice. This is the most public realm of stewardship. The advocacy may be focused on the environment, on fair treatment of a particular group of people, or wherever you find systemic injustice. How you and your family participate in this area of stewardship can range from sending e-mail or letters to a government official to speaking before a government committee.

Finally, all the decisions made along the way need to be brought together to be tested against the family's mission. The choices made about commitments of time, the use of natural resources, means of interacting with neighbors and community, methods of supporting and participating in the life of the church, and ways to seek justice all come together. Pulling together the various parts harmoniously is not a one-time decision. As children grow older, as jobs change, or as responsibilities for other family members intervene, the decisions require fresh examination.

Bible Stories and Spiritual Practices

Each chapter in this book focuses on one broad area of stewardship: the family's mission, stewardship in the family, stewardship in the congregation, stewardship in the community, and stewardship through seeking justice. Each chapter includes a brief look at two Bible passages: one from the Hebrew Scriptures and one from the New Testament. Also included in each chapter is the identification of a spiritual practice, chosen because it appears to be intrinsic to stewardship. The five spiritual practices are:

—Discernment
—Hospitality
—Generosity
—Fasting
—Advocacy for others

These practices provide a spiritual focus to this examination of stewardship. Unlike such spiritual practices as prayer, Bible reading, and meditation, these five are rarely used on a daily basis. However, they can be valuable habits to have at your disposal when needed. Be sure to include them as you work out your call to be God's stewards.

How to Use This Book

This book is designed to help you and your family think about your choices as stewards of God's world and word and how your faith enters into making those decisions. Include your whole family in the discussion. Being a part of such conversations is the best way to teach children about their role as stewards of God's world. Being included in the decision making will also help your children understand why certain choices are made, teaching your values in the midst of using them. Be aware, however, that your children may be sharp critics when values, decisions, and actions don't match.

The first part of the book contains chapters for participants, while the second part contains corresponding session guides for a group leader. If you are a group leader, be sure to read the chapters for participants as well as the leader's guide.

Expect to return to stewardship decisions again and again as you seek to be a family faithful to the God who has called you to be stewards of this world. The decisions you make this month will probably not be the ones you will make in ten years or perhaps in ten weeks. The circumstances of your economic life, the ages of your children, the health of each family member, and many other variables make each set of choices unique. What remains constant is your call to be God's faithful stewards, individually and together.

Many families find that discussing topics like stewardship seems countercultural and can be difficult to do alone. Consider inviting another family or two to join you in this discussion. The leader's guide of this book contains suggestions to help groups of adults and groups of families use this resource. The Christian faith is a faith of community. Rarely do we need that community more than when we seek to make changes in how we live that faith publicly. May you and your family benefit from this study, and may your understanding of yourselves as God's faithful people be enhanced.

Chapter One
Getting Started

What is stewardship? Once relegated to church discussions at money-raising time, the word *stewardship* is now used in the public realm, particularly with regard to how we treat the environment. Indeed, a broad understanding of stewardship for Christians takes us to a conversation about faithful choices: choices about work, home, finances, time, family, and persons or groups beyond the family. Certainly decisions about money, your money—that forbidden topic in polite company—is included in those choices, but it is not the beginning and the end of the discussion. For the purpose of this book, those choices relate to what is most important for one's family, how life is organized within the family, how the family relates to the church, how the family relates to the wider community, and, finally, how the family puts all those decisions and choices together to live faithful Christian lives in the twenty-first century. Stewardship, then, can be understood as how we use our resources—time, talents, and finances—to respond to God's love.

Let it be said first that family is interpreted broadly in this context. We define family, for the purpose of this book, primarily as parent(s) and child(ren) living at home, without attempting to identify the blood relationship or the number of adults and children. Some may consider adults who have chosen to live together to be a family (though I would use the term *household* for this designation). However, here we are concerned about how parents and children make and live out their choices to be God's faithful disciples of Jesus Christ. Of particular concern is how parents can be role models and educators of Christian stewardship.

Now that you see the big picture of stewardship and the intended audience, let's meet a family who will travel this journey with us. This family has two parents and two children. Along the way, we meet some of their friends. Our family consists of Mary and John Ingram and their children, Melissa (nine years old) and Jason (five years old). The Ingrams are active in their congregation. As their children have become more involved in activities outside the home, from church to school groups, new questions have arisen about giving to their congregation, spending time together as a family, and examining their financial picture. As they observe families with adolescent children, the Ingrams realize that those kinds of questions are only going to increase and become more complicated. We will listen in on their discussions and family meetings as they struggle with the issues raised in this book—issues that you are likely facing as well.

Our decision making through the eyes of God's stewards is smoother if we are clear about our commitment to faithful living. Without this foundational commitment, we easily fall into settling for pat answers for the decisions that face us. One mother discovered the need to keep the basic decisions before her and described her experience in this way:

> When my son Tobie was twelve years old, I left a stressful job and took a year off to bring my workaholic life back into balance. The decision was difficult because it had great economic consequences for our family. Doing without my income for a year would require us to make some drastic changes in our lifestyle, but we all agreed that it would be worth it. And indeed it was!
>
> During that year there were many times when Tobie was not sure that we had made the right decision. His need to have a mother who was less stressed and more available had been a primary consideration and he was all in favor of it—theoretically. But when I had said one too many times, "No, Tobie, you can't have/do (whatever) because we can't afford it," he was ready to retract his support.
>
> Several months into the year I heard myself saying those words *we can't afford it* yet again and what I actually was doing suddenly became clear. I had slipped into a comfortable pattern of explaining every no by reminding him of our limited financial resources, when the truth was that I would have said no to many of those requests even if our resources had been unlimited. No matter how much money we had, there were many things that this twelve-year-old wanted to have and do that were not supported by our values. I had to stop hiding behind an easy answer if I wanted Tobie to understand the commitments out of which our household was trying to live.[1]

Notice that the woman, Judith Smith, and her family had previously determined commitments for their family. Yet, even with those decisions in place, it was easy to forget that they were the basis for future decisions. Reviewing and restating the commitments regularly reminds us why we made them. Without that reminder, Judith found herself falling back on easy answers to requests from her son, answers that didn't remind him of those commitments. Thus, the first stop on this path to faithful living as God's stewards is the recognition of God's call to your family, whether there are two or ten family members, and the decision you make about how you accept and understand that call.

Joshua 24:1–28 and Mark 10:17–22

The matter of living faithfully takes us back to our earliest ancestors in the faith. A good place to begin is with leaders of the Israelites. Joshua was one such faithful leader. Chosen by God to be the leader as the Israelites moved into the promised land, he was taught by Moses, who knew that he himself would not be allowed to enter that land. The renewal of the call to Joshua and all of God's people in Joshua 24 came at the end of Joshua's life. In verse 29, we learn that he died at 110 years of age, old age being a mark of faithfulness to God. Turn to the Bible and read how one family, and then a whole people, accepted God's call in Joshua 24:1–28.

Look at the passage again, particularly at verses 14–27, the exchange

What do you think Joshua meant when he said, "but as for me and my household, we will serve the LORD" (Josh. 24:15)? What are the expectations of people who accept this call, according to Joshua?

between Joshua and the people. Allow Joshua's words to present God's call to you and your family. What call does your family acknowledge and accept? What is the basis for your call as stewards? Then, suggest that they come up with a word or phrase that they will keep with them for a few days as a reminder. Provide paper and markers for each person to write the word(s) so that they can look at them regularly. You might give each one a balsa wood disk, available at craft stores, and have family members write the words on one side of it. The disk will be sturdy enough to carry in a pocket or purse. Suggest that family members also think of a way that they will record the times when they were reminded of the story of Joshua.

During this week, when did the story from Joshua come to mind? How did it influence you during this time?

After a few days, bring the family together and hear their ideas about the story of Joshua and the Israelites. Then move to a story about Jesus, who also put the question of choice about serving God to the people he encountered. Perhaps his most disturbing encounter was with the rich man, a story included in Matthew, Mark, and Luke. Read it in Mark 10:17–22.

Now that you have the story in mind, read it spiritually, using an ancient method of pondering Scripture to hear its unique word to you. The purpose of this type of Scripture reading is to open yourself to God's Word. Rather than mine the words for hidden meanings, let the words flow over and within you so that they form you through God's spirit.

Before you begin, prepare yourself and a space for reading God's Word in this manner. Set aside about 30 minutes—less time if you are including elementary school–age children. (In that case, the adults may read the Scripture on their own at another time when they can spend more time on it, but you should still provide a shorter process for the entire family.) The Ingrams chose to follow the directions that follow (with a shortened time frame) for exploring Mark 10:17–22 with their children. If possible, unplug the telephone. Play soft instrumental music, if you wish. Have everyone breathe deeply several times to calm body, mind, and spirit.

What is God saying to you in these words? Where are you in this story? What prayers to God does this story draw from you?

First, invite everyone to think about this question: "God, what are you saying to me in these words?" Read Mark 10:17–22 aloud, slowly and reflectively. Take it one phrase or action at a time. Don't hurry. Pause for everyone to think about the words or phrases that caught their attention. If you wish, after a time of silence invite family members to name the words or phrases that held their attention.

Second, suggest that everyone think about the text and this question: "Where am I in this story?" This is a time to examine your own feelings, thoughts, desires, and hopes, and how they relate or are drawn to this text. Sometimes it is helpful to read the text aloud again. Maintain silence for a few moments. Again, invite family members to name how they found a connection with this story.

Third, have the family members speak to God regarding this text. Ask, "What prayers to God does this story draw from me?" It may lead to prayers of confession or of praise. It may lead to a conversation with God. Some family members may want to write down a prayer or a journal entry to capture their thoughts.

Finally, ask your family members to breathe deeply again and calm themselves as they come to rest in God.

The Ingrams were a bit surprised at the willingness of their children to stay with the process of Bible study, which lasted about twenty minutes. That night, after the children were asleep Mary and John reviewed the Joshua story, made their own balsa disks, and then took more time to read and reflect on the story from Mark.

In a few days, or whenever you decide the time is right, come together to discuss and explore the ideas that the stories of Joshua and the rich man have given you during this time. After a period of conversation and discernment, begin to put together the call that has come to your family. See page 13 for help with this discernment process. According to Marjorie Thompson, "Spiritual discernment is a vital process for children to learn, as it can help them make personal decisions throughout life. To use it in the family context also teaches that genuine discernment is a mutual process requiring a community of faith for confirmation."[2] We make many decisions daily—individually, with another family member, as an entire family—that do not require discernment. Some are quite simple, such as what to eat for breakfast or when to leave for work. Others take a little more time, such as selecting a birthday present or planning a dinner party. Still others have a big effect on family life and require more thought and care. It is such decisions, from making a career change to determining God's call for your family, that can be better made through the spiritual practice of discernment.

When you have chosen a sentence describing God's call for your family and have made something to help you remember it, pause to give thanks to God and to remember that God's presence and support will be with you for this journey. The litany format with a repeated response below allows younger children to participate easily. Use this prayer or adapt it to fit your family:

Leader: Gracious God, giver of the fullness of life, we seek your blessing as we struggle to be your people.

Response: Help us to live according to your word.

Leader: Gracious God, giver of the abundance of life, we seek to understand the true meaning of abundance.

Response: Help us to live according to your word.

Leader: Gracious God, giver of the comforts of life, we seek to recognize when we are comfortable enough.

Response: Help us to live according to your word.

Leader: Gracious God, giver of life, we give you thanks for all that you have given to us.

Response: Help us to live according to your word. Amen.

The whole Ingram family—John, Mary, Melissa, and Jason—participated in the discernment process. The children were allowed to come and go as they wished. Both children contributed to the selection of the sentence describing God's call to their family. The banner they created included a paint handprint of each family member.

Travelers along the Way

No family travels this stewardship road alone. Joshua's words from God were to all the people of Israel, and they responded with one voice. In his words to them, Joshua recalled the days of their ancestors as well. We travel with our faith family today and our faith family from years past, that whole "cloud of witnesses" that Paul reminds us of in Hebrews 12:1. Take a moment with your family to call forth memories of that group of ancestors who surround you.

That "cloud of witnesses" includes far more than the people we know or can name, of course. More than individual persons of faith, it is also a body of people. Read 1 Peter 2:4–10, seeking a sense of the people to which you belong. Discipleship in Christ is not a lonely vocation. We are bound together with other believers from all times and places, but we know particularly the bonds we have with those in our congregation. If you are reading this book on your own, look for other families who might partner with you in this endeavor to be good stewards of all God has given you. Your partnership can consist of anything from regular telephone conversations, to discussing each chapter of this book, to participating in mission projects together. Christianity is not a faith of one person; it is a faith given to a people. Therefore, it is strengthened when we are able to explore it with others.

At this point, consider whether you want to continue examining stewardship alone or whether you want to invite others to ponder these questions with you.

After conversation at the dinner table, Mary Ingram asked the children which people from their church they would like to know better. Later she and John selected a single parent, Lee Kim, with two children about the same age as Melissa and Jason, to invite to continue this examination of family and stewardship with them.

A Rule for Your Family

Earlier you read how Judith Smith came to realize the need for looking at decisions and how they are interpreted to family members. From there she moved to recognizing the need for household rules to keep her family on track. The word *rules* may have a sharp edge to your ears. Rules laid down by someone else, with little regard for those affected, is not what is meant here. Groups of religious people, from monasteries to communes, have found the need to establish a set of guidelines—sometimes called the order, or rule—which sets the tone and the expectations of the community for its members. This rule has at its core the central beliefs of the people and as its goal helping people live out these beliefs together. Without acceptance of and adherence to the rule, the group soon falls apart. This need for structure so that we might follow our call more faithfully is important for families too. This rule of life establishes the patterns necessary to make the regular habits of stewardship we determine a consistent part of our daily lives.

What rules, disciplines, or habits would help you stay on track or keep on the journey for your lives as God's stewards? What will be your family's rule? Here are Scripture mandates that Judith Smith and her family found helpful:

—Do not charge interest to the poor (Exod. 22:25). How can we make faithful decisions about borrowing and lending?
—Leave gleanings for others (Lev. 23:22). How is it that we can eat

and live responsibly so that all the world can eat?

—Practice tithing (2 Chr. 31:4–10). How do we understand the source of our money and how we spend it, all of it, not just what we give to the church?

—Practice hospitality (Heb. 13:2). How is it that we welcome others, especially those who are strangers and aliens?

—Keep the Sabbath (Deut. 5:12–15). How might we, as a family, put aside time on a regular basis, or refrain from ordinary activities, to acknowledge that we belong to God? [3]

This list does not exhaust the household rules important for your family. And you need not connect each one to a Bible reference. Look at the areas and the examples below. Select one and think about a rule in that area that might benefit your family. Talk about it together. Consensus is important if you expect everyone to pay attention to the rule you create.

Use of material resources

—We will work toward less use of things that cannot be recycled.
—We will carpool to work.
— (Create your own rules.)

Time to worship God individually, as a family, and with the congregation

—We will pray together daily.
—We will make congregational worship a family activity.
— (Create your own rules.)

Use of financial resources

—We will allocate to charity and church first as we plan our budget.
—We will set aside all charity requests other than our church pledge and review them quarterly.
— (Create your own rules.)

Use of time and energy to help others

—We will serve together at a soup kitchen monthly.
—We will volunteer in the church nursery as a family.
— (Create your own rules.)

Use of time and energy for the good of the family

—We will reserve Friday night as family night.
—We will plan at least one special event together a month.
— (Create your own rules.)

At this point, just jot down ideas and notes. Brainstorm alone or with your children. (Remember that *everything* is written down in brainstorming; evaluation of ideas comes later.) Keep the list, without changes, as you work through the rest of this book. You will be building your household rule as you read and discuss each chapter.

The Ingrams invited the Kims for Sunday lunch. Although Mary had an initial conversation with Lee Kim, they explained further their goal to be faithful stewards of God's gifts to them and invited Lee and his children to join them. The two families agreed to meet on a regular basis to discuss and work with issues around families and stewardship. Melissa showed the Kims their family banner. When the children went off to play, the adults explored the possibility further. Lee Kim said that he and his children would study the Exodus and Mark passages on their own and make their family banner. That afternoon the adults brainstormed rules in the categories listed earlier. This helped them get to know one another and prepared them to begin chapter 2 together.

Summary

As Christians, we are called by God to be faithful stewards of God's creation. This call comes to us individually and to us as families. While the call is the same to all, it is also unique to each person and family. One method for discovering this unique call is to read the Word of God spiritually. Once families have discerned their call for this time and place, they are ready to begin the journey of discovering how they live out this call faithfully. Included in this faithful living is the establishment of a rule of life for their family, a rule that will help them form the habits needed to be faithful to their call. The remaining chapters in this book will help you develop a rule of life for your family, one that encourages you to live as faithful disciples in this time and place and be good stewards of all that God has given you.

Coming to an Important Decision Together

1. State the arena for the decision you are pondering. Say it in a neutral form, such as "What is God's call to our family?"

2. Agree that this is a decision that you want to make as a family. Get clear agreement about this from each family member.

3. Together, brainstorm the possible answers to the question. Include answers based solely on your real lives as well as the emotional aspects that come forth as you try to answer the question.

4. Individually, think about the list you created. Pray for God's help as you decide which possibilities you think hold the most promise for your family. Try to let go of personal prejudices (either the idea you like the best or the one you like the least) as you do this.

5. Come together and seek a consensus for a family choice. Keep talking until you have reached a consensus. If necessary, take a break for individual reflection, but set a time when you will come back together.

6. Once you have a choice, test it for a while before making it permanent— at least for now.

You may wish to use the words of Scripture or to put your call from God into your own words. Write one that all family members can say with some degree of understanding. Make a small poster that everyone signs or adds an initial or symbol of assent to, or find some other way to create a visual reminder of God's call as your family knows it. Display it where your family will see it regularly. Here is a sample of one way this could look.

Chapter 2
At Home

Once you have an idea of the particular call to your family, the next step is to figure out what the choice means for your daily life together. Keep in mind, though, that your life changes as family members grow older and as the configuration of the family is modified. Therefore, the choices made today surely will be altered at a later date. For now, however, the next step is to examine how you make space for and structure family time. In other words, how are you the stewards of the time that you spend together as a family? Many factors influence your family time. You can make your own list; here are just a few factors that might be on it:

— Children in different schools
— Commuting parents
— Arrangements for child care
— Parents who work alternating shifts
— Sports or other after-school or weekend activities
— Volunteer responsibilities
— Aging parents

In this chapter, the focus is on the day-to-day activities of families along with those activities that occur occasionally or annually. One way to get a handle on the day-to-day activities is to look at your calendar for the past month. What rhythm of family time do you see? Does it build toward the weekend? Is it concentrated on a particular day? Can you discern a pattern? A framework of substance for Christian families is the church year. Thus, one activity appropriate to this chapter is an exploration of the church year and how you can incorporate it naturally into your family's activities.

> Who is the Moses in your family? What might Jethro say about the way your family works together?

Exodus 18:13–16 and Luke 10:38–42

Important to the stewardship of time together as a family is how you work together and who shoulders which responsibilities. Two very different stories from the Bible can help us move into that conversation. Turn first to Exodus 18. Moses and the Israelites have escaped from slavery in Egypt. It seems that Moses had sent his wife, Zipporah, and their two sons to stay with Jethro, Zipporah's father, when conditions got a little shaky. Now the Israelites are camped near Mount Sinai, and Jethro has sent a message to Moses that he is coming to visit and returning to Moses his wife and sons.

> When are you the Martha in your family? When are you the Mary?

On that first night, Moses told Jethro, who is a priest of Midian, all that Yahweh had done. Upon hearing such good news, Jethro offered sacrifices to Yahweh. Read verses 13 through 26, which describe what happened the next morning. After giving his sage advice and watching as Moses follows it, Jethro exits and is never heard from again. A new system of operations is in place. Isn't it curious that someone who apparently worshiped other gods as well as Yahweh was the one to point out the need for a different approach to Yahweh's chosen leader?

The other story you want to consider comes from the Gospel of Luke. Turn to chapter 10 and read verses 38–42. Once more it seems that one family member is doing all the work. This story has given readers, particularly women, a hard time for many years. It is easy to hear Jesus' words as a scolding for Martha, while Mary gets off easy. Bible interpreters have more recently pointed out that Jesus isn't so much scolding Martha as affirming the place of women as learners, a concept that would have been alien to his culture and to the early readers of Luke's Gospel. At the same time, Martha did have to worry about the food for her dinner guests, likely a dozen or more. No deli around the corner or home-delivery pizza was available to her. The story ends with Jesus' words. What do you think happened next?

Leaders, helpers, workers, and learners—each role is necessary in a family. Think about each story. How does one complement the other? Together what do they suggest to you about the way your family might work together? Take a few moments for silent reflection on these stories. Then talk about them together. Let your conversation be open to and opened by God's Spirit. Wait for the Spirit to give you words to say. Don't be afraid of silence together.

When the Ingrams and the Kims met again, they first read the Bible stories. Lee Kim had little to say initially. Finally, he opened up, telling of his wife's death from cancer and the loneliness that surrounded him. He acknowledged that these stories and questions about working together as a family were painful, for he had all the responsibility now. The differences between the two families were stark. No one knew what to say. Then, eight-year-old Rachel Kim said, "Dad, David and I can help too." Her sincerity touched each adult, and now they were able to move on.

Time Together

Every year or so, it seems, a study comes out that says that the family meal together is nearly extinct. What was once a daily ritual, perhaps three times a day, is found only occasionally in most families. Much could be said about the importance of sitting at table together, but that is not the only indication of family life gone wrong or disappeared. A Roper Starch Worldwide poll in the late 1990s reported that, on average, Americans shop six hours a week and spend only forty minutes playing with their children. These are just two indications of the need to plan family time together.

Being a family, something more than just an intergenerational group that lives at the same address, is nearly impossible if you do not talk, work, and have fun together. As already noted, the constraints on family time are many, but the necessity for being together is just as clear today as it was for any generation past.

> During this week, pay attention to who is the leader, the worker, the helper, and the learner in your family. How are these roles shared?

Many families have found that establishing a "family night" each week helps carve out time to be with one another. Just one evening a week is no small feat in today's busy schedules, whether you are six or thirty-six. Dorothy Bass, in *Receiving the Day,* tells of fourth-grade children who are required by the school system to purchase datebooks: "Not just the little pamphlet calendars printed by greeting card companies. . . . But datebooks, like the ones business executives often carry."[1] It probably goes without saying, but finding that evening is more difficult when there are teenagers in the household or when a parent commutes long distances to work.

This lack of time together has not gone unnoticed, however. Communities as far apart as Wayzata, Minnesota, and Ridgewood, New Jersey, have had annual "family nights." All sports practices, community events, and even homework were canceled for the evening. Television sets were blank as families talked and played games together.[2] The events of September 11, 2001, and the 2003 Iraq war reminded us that family life is important. However, once the trauma is gone, so too is our fervent intent to improve our time together. Being a family takes planning and commitment.

Certainly there are times when having just one meal together each week is a major scheduling feat, and every plan needs fallback positions. However, the earlier you begin the habit of clearing one evening free for family, the stronger the impetus will be as your children grow older. One family may declare Friday nights as their night together and turn off the television to eat dinner together and play games or read a book aloud. Another may find that Sunday afternoon is the best time and plan brunch out after church with a trip to a sculpture garden or museum to complete the day. Still another may gather with their extended family for Sunday dinner, rotating the meal among their homes or selected restaurants. The important thing is not to give up if it doesn't happen for a week or two or if your first attempts fall flat. Think of it as practice; indeed, it is the spiritual practice of hospitality to one another. When you want to play a musical instrument, you must practice. Learning to play the simplest melody requires practicing it over and over. You progress to more complicated melodies. Even when you think you have a piece of music down cold, you can mess up. But you don't give up the instrument because you made one mistake. Don't give up the stewardship of family time together because it doesn't work at first or because events

out of your control cause you to miss the appointed time.

As the Ingrams and the Kims talked about a family time each week, they decided to keep free the same time they had chosen to meet together each month. Then they talked about what each family might do on its own. The children gave their ideas: go to the zoo, play games, go to a ball game. Lee Kim observed that he and his children were frequently home together, but they would plan more intentionally what they would do with this time now set apart. John Ingram noted that often when they were home with their children, each family member was involved in an individual activity. Mary Ingram expressed a desire that their family might read a book aloud together. All these ideas were recorded for each family to plan its special time together.

The Church Year and the Stewardship of Family Time

To prepare for a broader examination of the stewardship of family time, list the family birthdays, anniversaries, and other special occasions that your family celebrates every year. Then add those special events and holidays that your family normally celebrates.

The church year provides a structure for family time on a regular basis, and perhaps on a schedule that even now exists for your family. Many families already light the candles on the Advent wreath each week during Advent, when they pray and read Scripture together. Building on an existing plan that works is usually better than starting in a new and foreign place. What might you do during Lent that follows a similar pattern? Look at "The Church Year" on page 24. Talk together about ways you can begin to build family routines and traditions around specific times in it. To find new seasonal activities, consider learning about the heritage of your family and the traditions from that history.

This process will help you see the potential for the church year to help you engage with the stewardship of your family life.

1. On a large sheet of paper or several small sheets, print the seasons of the church year and include special religious days that your congregation observes. Begin with "The Church Year" on page 24. Leave lots of space under each season or special day.

2. Transfer the family birthdays, anniversaries, and other occasions that you listed earlier to the corresponding places on the church year chart. Now add special events family members will observe during the coming year, such as graduating from school, beginning a new school, getting a first driver's license, or reading their first chapter book. Leave space to write under them too.

3. With a colored pen or marker, write under each occasion the way your family marks that event together. For example, "We read the Christmas story

from Luke before dinner on Christmas" or "We each say a sentence prayer for the birthday person." When you have finished, take turns reading it aloud. You may be surprised to see that you already do many things together. (Another time you might evaluate how those things are done and how everyone can participate more fully.) You may notice that some seasons are heavy with activity while other seasons are bare.

4. Brainstorm ways that your family might mark any occasions listed on the chart. Use a different colored pen or marker from the one used earlier. One person can record all the ideas, or each person can write his or her own ideas. Set a time limit. When time is up, read what has been written.

5. Take a break. Have a snack together or go outdoors for a game of Frisbee. (This is not a time for a parent to make a few phone calls or a child to head to the computer.)

6. Come back to the chart. Ask for other ideas that anyone wants to add to it.

7. Look at the current month and one or two months that follow it. Ask, "How might our family mark some of the events on the chart during these months?" (Be clear that you are not going to mark every occasion or do everything that has been suggested. You want to plan for

those times that make sense to celebrate as a family.)

8. After the months that you planned have ended, come together to talk about how it went. Based on that conversation, plan for the next two or three months.

Both the Kims and the Ingrams had a good time creating their charts. For their break, they had a snack outdoors. When they returned to their charts, each family learned of differing holiday customs and expressed eagerness to celebrate some of these times together.

More than the Time Together

The stewardship of family life is not just about the time the family spends together. It is also about how we support one another so that each family member can be a constructive member of the community and the congregation. Sometimes this means taking on more household tasks so that one family member can accept a volunteer responsibility. This might be a good time to review the choices about God's call that you made as you read and worked with the material in chapter 1.

An important aspect of hospitality in family life is how the tasks that maintain family life are ordered and accomplished. In other words, who takes out the garbage? Who sees that there is milk in the refrigerator? Who maintains the family calendar? How are all the tasks accomplished that

keep the day-to-day life of each family member and your life together intact? Some tasks are clearly the responsibility of the adults in the family. I doubt that you want to relegate paying the bills or selecting an insurance policy to a child. However, many tasks, from dusting the furniture to emptying the dishwasher, can be taken on by family members of various ages. Your first task is to list the jobs that would be appropriate for all or most members of your family. Then decide how to divide them and when you will switch them around. Yes, switching them around is important to keep monotony or boredom from setting in, not to mention that cry "But I *always* have to . . ."

One family writes each job on a slip of paper and puts the papers in a jar. On Saturday morning, each family member draws a paper from the jar until all the papers have been taken. If one family member has unusual responsibilities outside the household over the weekend, the numbers of papers that person draws is adjusted. Since these are primarily household-maintenance chores, the deadline for finishing is the end of the weekend, unless the person negotiates a different deadline with the family. When the drawing is over, pray together that the tasks will be done for the good of the family and that family members may live a life of faithful discipleship.

Another family, with younger children, lists the jobs on a sheet of paper. The three children get to select a specified number of chores and print their initials next to the ones they choose. Most of these jobs are daily chores or tasks that are done two or more times during the week, such as putting the newspapers in the recycling bin or setting the table. In this way, the children have the possibility of different jobs each week. The parents take other jobs on the list, and they too put initials next to those tasks. A birthday gives a child the privilege of selecting from a wider variety of tasks marking a new level of maturity.

As the Ingrams and the Kims worked with this material, each family planned its own way to distribute chores and responsibilities. When the children went off to play, Lee Kim spoke: "The sole responsibility of caring for my children sometimes takes me to the end of my rope. I have no family members nearby, and there is just never a break." He went on to say that he was worried about the lack of individual time he had with each child. Mary Ingram silently decided to invite Rachel and David for play dates with Melissa and Jason on a regular basis.

The Family as Conserver of Family Stories

A final task for the stewardship of family life is passing on stories of the family, its ancestors, and its faith. On his deathbed, Moses told the people of Israel, "Take to heart all the words that I am giving in witness against you today; give them as a command to your children, so that they may diligently observe all the words of the law. This is no trifling matter for you, but rather your very life" (Deut. 32:46–47). These "words of the law" were not limited to codes and restrictions but included the history of the covenant community and its relationship with God. Both are important to pass on to our children. We Christians of the twenty-first century have many, many stories of God's presence and work in this universe to tell our children, from stories in the Bible to those of faithful people today. Beyond these stories of the faith, we have our family narratives to help our children know who they are and who they can be.

At this point, focus on ways to introduce your children to members of their family, those living today and those of generations past. Here are some things you might do:

— Look through photograph albums or watch family videos. As you do so, pause to tell family stories.
— Ask elderly relatives to record childhood memories by writing them down or making an audiotape. Knowing the stories of the past will bind you together as a family.
— Write a letter together to family members who live miles away. Phone calls and e-mail are fast, but nothing is more thoughtful than a letter from the whole family. Drawings from young children can be included.
— Visit cemeteries where relatives are buried or neighborhoods where they lived.
— Tell your children about family traditions that have been passed down from generation to generation, anything from favorite family bedtime snacks to holiday rituals.

After discussing ways to pass on family stories, the Kims and the Ingrams were anxious to try some of the suggestions. Lee Kim was especially aware of his need and desire to help his children remember and learn more about their mother.

Your Family and Your Congregation

Finally, as you plan family time, connect your family to your congregation. When you pray together, include prayers for your congregation as well as for individual members and the church staff. Include in your family time worshiping together with the congregation. Invite church members to share in your family time once in a while. Many families have found surrogate grandparents, aunts, and uncles in this way and have made family life and congregational life richer for everyone. You'll read more about families, stewardship, and congregational life in chapter 3.

> What family rule might grow out of your search for a fixed family time?

Lee Kim and John and Mary Ingram pondered ways for their families to be more closely connected to their congregation. They began planning a joint dinner to which they would invite some congregational members. Life was looking brighter for each family.

A Prayer for Stewardship of Family Life

Leader: Welcoming God, arms open to all, we enter into your wonderful hug.

Response: Hold us tightly in your love.

Leader: Welcoming God, arms open to all, we seek to care for each family member (*or say each person's name*).

Response: Hold us tightly in your love.

Leader: Welcoming God, arms open to all, we seek to welcome others into our family circle.

Response: Hold us tightly in your love.

Leader: Welcoming God, arms open to all, we give you thanks for the love of family and congregation.

Response: Hold us tightly in your love. Amen.

Summary

We, with our children, are formed into a family by the commitments and practices we adopt together. Being good stewards of God's creation begins in the family unit and in the home. One helpful construct for planning our family time is the church year. Through it we can plan our time together and incorporate ways to pass on the stories of faith and family ancestors. At the same time, each family must figure out a way to accomplish the tasks necessary to family life. Time, tasks, and stories are important components of the stewardship life that exists around the family. Through these activities, we practice hospitality toward one another and together toward others, the next step in our stewardship growth.

The Church Year

Advent (begins four Sundays before Christmas Day)

The Twelve Days of Christmas

Epiphany (January 6)

Ordinary Time (the Sundays between Epiphany and Lent)

Lent (forty days—not including Sundays—beginning with Ash Wednesday)

Holy Week (Palm Sunday through Easter)

Easter

Pentecost (the Sunday fifty days after Easter)

Ordinary time (the Sundays between Pentecost and Advent)

The Practice of Hospitality and Family Time

A hospitable home, one welcoming to each family member and to others, is the backbone for the stewardship of family life. In *Soul Feast*, Marjorie Thompson writes, "Parents provide a hospitable home by being genuinely present to their children—available to listen, affirm, guide, and correct."[3] We learn about hospitality as we are treated with respect and made welcome, whether by our own family or our congregation or in new places. Undergirded with a hospitable home—at least an attempt to provide it—the family is strengthened to participate in the spiritual practice of hospitality:

- —As its members interact with one another
- —As its members joyfully engage in random acts of kindness
- —As it invites others beyond the family to join them for meals or other activities
- —As it prays for others, known and not known personally to them
- —As it seeks to expand its care for others
- —As it seeks to welcome people who are different from them

In our culture and time, the ways of practicing hospitality are many. We practice it as we do quiet, thoughtful acts for individual family members or friends. We practice it as we advocate for those who cannot advocate for themselves. We practice it as we gather at the Lord's Table and greet everyone there in Christian love. As such, the spiritual practice of hospitality holds a family together even when its members are apart.

Chapter 3
At Church

As indicated in the previous chapter, stewardship within the family has a close connection to the stewardship of that family within the congregation. The Ingram family looked to their congregation first for another family to broaden their discussions and to provide mutual support during this study. Thus, it is only natural that we turn from the stewardship within the *family* to stewardship within the *congregation*. How we approach stewardship in the area of our church membership has two parts: giving and serving. Including children and young people in both acts of giving

and acts of serving, according to research, makes for a better chance that in adulthood they will:

— Volunteer
— Be involved in the community
— Participate in political activities
— Believe they can make a difference[1]

In other words, they will become citizens who care not only about themselves but also about their community and the people who live there. They will grow up with a sense of hope that allows them to work on sticky problems. They will be the adults you would want your children to be.

In order for the stewardship of your family to be effective within the church, your children, whatever their age, will need to feel that they are a part of, and a contributing member to, your congregation. Providing occasions for your children to participate with you in projects serving others and involving your children in how you give to others and your congregation, along with providing opportunities for your children to get to know other adults in the church, will go a long way toward providing them with a sense of belonging. Each of these occasions is discussed in this chapter.

Deuteronomy 15:7–11 and John 12:1–8

Much in the Bible, of course, commends serving and giving to others. However, the passages selected for this chapter include those acts that reflect generosity in particular.

Looking first at Deuteronomy, we find an admonishment to give ungrudgingly to those who are needy. According to biblical scholar Patrick Miller, the motivation for generosity to the powerless is the memory of slavery in Egypt that the Israelites carried with them.[2] They knew well what it was like to be

---

From your conversation and thinking about Moses and the Israelites, what does generosity mean for God's people?

---

worked to the bone. Once the straw was given to them to make bricks; they now had to gather the straw and still produce the same number of bricks. No longer slaves of the pharaoh, in their thankfulness for being brought out of slavery they would serve and give to others.

1. Read Deuteronomy 15:7–11 aloud. What words suggest generosity to you?

   _____

   _____

   _____

2. Read those verses aloud again. Who are the recipients of this generosity?

   _____

   _____

   _____

Look at the verses once more. This time, search for words that specify parts of the body. Notice how they reinforce the idea that attitude and actions are expected to work together. One does not give food with the hands and refuse to look at the recipient, suggesting an unworthiness of that person. One does not look upon the thirsty child and speak words of encouragement but give no cup of water.

Do you remember the story of the rich man in Luke 10:25–37 who asked Jesus what he must do to inherit heaven? Here was a devout Jew who followed all the rules, those same rules in Deuteronomy. In answering him, Jesus acknowledged God's law, that the man was to care for his family and neighbor. However, Jesus pushed through the understanding of the term *neighbor* to widen it to *include* rather than *exclude*. One wonders what the man, this one who studied the Torah, did. Or the rich man in Mark 10. He turned his back on Jesus when Jesus told him to give what he had to people who were poor. For Jesus, the Deuteronomic code still stands, expanded but intact. God's people are to help anyone in need and to do it with generous minds and hearts.

Perhaps as you read Deuteronomy something about verse 11 sounded familiar to you. In the story of Mary anointing Jesus in the Gospel of John, Jesus used the same words about those who are poor. Turn to John 12 now and read verses 1–8. We met Mary and Martha in chapter 2 of this study. We know about their brother Lazarus, Jesus' good friend, whom he raised from death. Here Martha is still serving food. Lazarus is sitting at table with Jesus. Can't you picture the scene? Good friends, good food, good conversation.

Then Mary enters with a hugely expensive jar of perfumed nard. The jar probably cost a year's wages for the common worker. Where Mary got the money for it, we don't know. She breaks open the jar and anoints Jesus' feet. "The house was filled with the fragrance of the perfume." This sentence alone points out the extravagance of Mary's act. The entire house was filled.

Judas's argument that the money should have been given to the poor prompted a response from Jesus. In doing so, he recalled Deuteronomy 15:11. Surely the guests present would have recognized those words as well.

> What else in the story points to Mary's extravagance and generosity?

Think about both passages: Deuteronomy 15:7–11 and John 12:1–8. How do they provide examples of serving and giving? Together, how do they exemplify generosity?

Generosity

In Galatians 5:22, being generous is called a "fruit of the Spirit." Generosity, then, is a spiritual practice, one borne out in serving and giving. As we serve, we use our time and talents to provide acts of mercy and to work for social action. When we give, we share our financial resources and material goods so that others can use them, particularly those who are in need or are powerless to provide for themselves. The connecting thread in these two parts of generosity is concern for others. There are many reasons that we might care for others: to relieve our guilt, to assure our personal and family safety, to secure a positive image of our public self, or even to gain something for ourselves. The teachings of the Bible, however, go

> How would you recognize an act that was done without a grudging heart? When have you experienced or seen an act of extravagance for someone else or for yourself?

beyond such personal reasons. We are instructed by word and example to serve with an open hand, willingly, and to give liberally, not with a grudging heart. With Mary as one model for us, we are to give and serve with extravagance.

As the Kim and Ingram families read and discussed the passages from Deuteronomy and John, they pondered the meaning of giving liberally with a loving heart for their families. Mary had grown up in the church and her family had always pledged. She was sure of this because she remembered the offering envelope her father placed in the offering plate each Sunday morning. However, money—not how much they had or how much they gave—was ever discussed with the children. For that matter, their family, though very active in the governing and workings of the congregation, had never talked about service, the giving of time and talents. Perhaps it was a simpler time then, she thought, and the role of each parent was more clearly defined; maybe the conversations didn't even happen between her parents.

John Ingram was amazed at the examples his children named as they answered the question about acts of extravagance. His daughter told of a classmate who shared her morning snack with another classmate. When questioned a bit further, Melissa explained that the snackless classmate was new and lived in the motel at the edge of town, the motel where homeless families were housed. He shook his head and muttered to himself, "And I thought we could keep them sheltered from the difficulties of the world. I had no idea she knew about homeless families here or the motel on the other side of town."

Lee Kim looked at the Ingrams and said, "You have shown an extravagance of caring to us as you include us in these conversations and in other times of your family life."

The children went to the kitchen to make popcorn while the adults continued the discussion of how they might more generously offer their time, talents, and financial resources to the church and the community. They also wondered how to nurture generosity in their children, especially in today's "me first" culture.

Opportunities for Giving and Serving

As in any spiritual practice, generosity does not become a part of your faith and life if you do not seek opportunities when you can practice it. Many such opportunities exist; we highlight three types in this chapter:

—Giving time to the congregation
—Using talents for serving
—Giving financial resources to the congregation and others

If you are working through this book at home with your family, you might talk about one category during a family meeting and then find a way to give and serve generously through it before taking up another category.

To prepare for your study of giving and serving generously, create a calendar for the previous four weeks on a large sheet of paper.

When the Congregation Gathers

At the top of the list of the time your family gives to your congregation when it gathers should be attending the weekly service of worship. While you may not have thought of it as giving time, and perhaps that is not the primary way to classify it, gathering with other church members to worship and pray is one way that you say by your actions that the life of your congregation is important to you and your family. You allot your family time to be a part of it and to support others through your presence. On the calendar for the past four weeks, block out the times your family *together* worshiped with your congregation.

Congregations come together as one body or in smaller groups for study, service, and fellowship. How does your family allot time to such gatherings of your faith community? Focus first on the times when you are together, not segregated into age groups. Perhaps you went to a potluck supper or an intergenerational program. List those times on the four-week calendar. The opportunities for a cross-age, family gathering will differ depending on the size of the congregation and the types of programs and ministries offered. Your decisions about how and when your family participates will change as children grow older, as work situations alter, and for a variety of other circumstances. If there are adolescents in your family, going to the youth group may be important to them. Add this to your calendar, but mark it with the initials of those participating in that activity. Add other congregational activities, such as church school or choir rehearsal, that individual family members participate in and put their initials next to the activities.

Here are questions you should consider as you ponder your family's stewardship through participation in congregational activities:

— How is our participation divided over activities of worship, study, service, and fellowship?
— Where are opportunities for our family to participate together in any of these activities?

When the Congregation Serves

The ministry areas of your congregation probably offer a number of opportunities for your family to serve others, within and outside the church membership. Most congregations have more opportunities for individuals, youth or adults, to participate in service than for families to do this together. Often, however, children can be included in service if adults give thought in advance to the children's participation in a project.

Think back over the past four weeks and identify times that your family, through your congregation, served others. Did you work together in a soup kitchen? Did you take a bag of groceries to the food pantry? Did you sort through clothes for a clothing drive? Did you deliver flowers to an elderly member of your congregation? Add these occasions to your calendar. If one family member did any of these things alone or with someone other than a family member, add them to your calendar but put the person's initials next to the description.

Too often we limit our children's experiences unnecessarily. A mother of a twelve-year-old son reported at a parents' group about a time when she was scheduled to serve at the soup kitchen. It was a school day and she planned to go with two other adults. An early-morning snowstorm canceled her son's school that day. She, her son, two other adults, and another child drove to the neighboring city to serve the noon meal. "My family helped out there on a Saturday last summer," she said, "but I think it was more impressive for my son to see that little children came during the week too."

Another family, parents and daughters (three and five years old), volunteered to serve the evening meal at a hospitality center where homeless families came for shelter and to spend the night. The girls played and ate with the children. They also helped serve and clean up. Even though the parents chose not to discuss why the families were sleeping at the church (and the girls wanted to sleep over too), these children had the experience of serving and feeding strangers.

Aside from opportunities for your family to serve in a congregational ministry together, a family member may be called to serve in a ministry because of that person's gifts or talents. For example, Mary Ingram was invited to serve on the education committee of their congregation. This would involve an evening meeting each month as well as work between meetings. Rachel Kim wanted to join the church choir that Melissa Ingram was in. For her father, this created the logistical problem of getting her there. In each case, other family members might be called on to change their routine or take on additional responsibilities in order for one member to participate in a new activity.

Discerning when to accept an invitation to serve, even though the invitation is to one family member, takes the thinking and prayers of the entire family. The family's schedule for the nights of the committee meetings would require adjustment in the case of the Ingrams. How could the other family members make this service possible for Mary? How could they help her decide whether this was a call from God or whether the work of the education committee was a match for her gifts and talents? Similar questions could be asked about Rachel's desire to be in the children's choir.

Consider these questions as you ponder your family's stewardship through participation in congregational service ministries:

— How does your family already participate in works of service through your congregation?
— In order for any family member to accept a new invitation of service, what might the rest of your family do?

When the Congregation Gives

One aspect of stewardship to the congregation is serving, but the other is giving—the giving away of one's money. The role of the family in nurturing children to be generous financial stewards cannot be underplayed. Just as children and young people who grow up serving continue those practices in their adult lives, children and young people who gave financially continue that generosity as adults.

In my career as a church educator, I have seen sophisticated youth budgets, complete with pledge cards and envelopes, fall by the wayside, and with good reason. Too often more effort was put into recording the nickels and dimes than was spent in explaining why the offerings were made and how they contributed to service and ministry. However, we got rid of everything and did nothing to encourage children and young people to think about the money they had. As a result, we have at least one generation of nongivers in the church. Now we are trying to help this generation of children-turned-adults to understand that we give out of our thankfulness to God rather than from our abundance or what is left over when all other bills are paid. The Bible stories about money and wealth, and there are many, do not exempt anyone from giving—not the poorest of the land or the richest, not women or men, not adults or children.

If you did not give financially as a child, you may wonder why we are concerned about the stewardship of money for children and young people. Some people argue that children have no money of their own so giving doesn't really mean anything to them. For children, the issue is not the money but the act and the message that giv-

ing is a spiritual practice for everyone, whatever their age or resources. It is a matter of full inclusion into Christ's church.

I have heard more than one story of a little girl in times past who carried coins in a knotted handkerchief to put into the offering plate on Sunday morning. A survey of books about money and children found precious little about generosity or even philanthropy. According to these authors, money not immediately spent on one's self was to be put into savings accounts or invested for one's future. Being generous to others wasn't even on the radar screen.

As for young people and disposable income, advertisements today give us a clue. Young people are one of the major advertising markets in affluent countries. The disposable income they have often is spent on compact discs, movies, fast food, and clothing. They too need the challenge of giving from what they have.

You may wonder how you might reconcile giving for your children when you already give. Each family will figure that out in its own way. If you grew up giving, you already know the importance of taking part in that congregational act. Here are just two examples that may spark others in your mind. When I was a child, my congregation had a Joash chest march on the first Sunday of the month. The money went to the upkeep of the little church. Although my siblings and I had our money for Sunday school, we were also given an offering for the Joash chest. We walked forward proudly, beginning long before we knew what money was, and had to be lifted up to drop our coins in the slot of the black metal box, then taking our place among the whole congregation. The amount is not critical, but taking part in giving is for all ages. Or consider this example. As a reminder of the many people in our world who live with hunger daily, some families have a small bowl or bank on the dining table. At each meal, two pennies are placed in the bowl at the end of the mealtime grace. This money is given to a hunger fund.

Many families begin the nurturing of stewardship giving when their children receive an allowance. Banks (often glass or plastic jars) are labeled for the various uses of the allowance: church, savings, treats, and school lunch. When the allowance is received, it is divided among the various banks. This type of arrangement provides many opportunities for talking about stewardship of money with children. One boy, about eight, asked to make a pledge during the annual congregational stewardship campaign. He reasoned that he was setting aside an amount each week and should have a way to make a pledge as his parents did. Fortunately, the church accommodated him, complete with a pledge card and envelopes. Jewish children are given a tzedakah box, in which they place money to give to others. You might adopt this practice for your home. Family offerings, such as the One Great Hour of Sharing offering during Lent, are often observed, but in this way you highlight giving any time during the church year.

As children grow older, you will want to include them in discussions about the family pledge, even if they are expected to make their own offering. Don't make conversations with your children about money scarcer than conversations about sexuality!

Consider these questions as you ponder your family's stewardship through participation in giving financially to your congregation:

—What are the opportunities for our family to talk about our financial gifts to our congregation?

—What help might we want from our congregation and our church staff to engage our children in these conversations and practices?

A Prayer for Our Stewardship at Church

Leader: Generous God, seeking abundance for all, we give heartfelt thanks for all that you have given us.

Response: Give us generous hearts.

Leader: Generous God, seeking abundance for all, we give heartfelt thanks for all to whom you have called us to serve.

Response: Give us generous hearts.

Leader: Generous God, seeking abundance for all, we give you heartfelt thanks for all you give us to share with others.

Response: Give us generous hearts. Amen.

Summary

While giving from our financial resources to the congregation is an important part of family stewardship, we cannot overlook the other avenues for generosity toward others available to children, young people, and adults through the congregation. As we teach and lead by example through acts of giving and serving, we stand in a long tradition of God's people whose hearts and hands are

> What additions will you make to your "family rule" regarding generosity?

opened to others. May our children say in adulthood, as Mister Rogers said, "My parents and grandparents were generous givers and gracious receivers. They made charity and service central in our family by their example and by letting us know in many ways how much that was valued by them."[3]

Ways to Nurture Generosity

1. As a family, commit to the well-being of others. How can you make this commitment visible in word and deed?

2. Include your children in congregational life. How might your children be more closely aligned with the faith community through activities and events of your congregation?

3. Make acts of giving and serving an expectation of both you and your children. How are you a role model for your children, and how are they an example to you?

4. Look for a variety of opportunities for your family to practice giving. What do you do now, and what else might you do?

5. Also look for opportunities for your family to practice serving. What do you do now, and what else might you do?

6. Connect acts of giving and serving to teachings from the Bible and the tradition. When might your family reflect on the acts of giving and serving that you do together or separately?

7. Find support for nurturing generosity through other families in your congregation. Where might you find families who will work on nurturing generosity with you so that you support one another?

8. Help the adults in your congregation live out the baptismal or dedication vows for your children. How might you provide ways for caring adults to get to know your children and your children to know them?

Based on "Eight Keys to Nurturing Generosity" from *Growing Up Generous: Engaging Youth in Giving and Serving,* by Eugene C. Roehlkepartain, Elanah Dalyah Naftali, and Laura Musegades (Bethesda, Md.: Alban Institute, 2000), chapters 6 and 7. The questions are the author's.

Chapter 4
In the Community

As you move out into communities beyond family and friends, you come to the city or town where you reside and beyond. The people you meet and the contacts you have with other cultures may differ from families in other places, but it is surely wider than the people two or three generations ago might have encountered where you live. How, as stewards of God's creation, will you interact with people and creation beyond your immediate family and your faith community? As you know more about people in other countries, how will you use natural resources so that there

is enough for everyone? As your family ponders such questions in this chapter, be open to a shift in your perception of God's world and your place in it.

Exodus 16:1-30 and Luke 11:3

Can you picture them? This forlorn-looking tribe of Israelites who, against all odds, escaped from slavery in Egypt. The food—that unleavened bread they packed as they made their hasty departure—is gone. The water ran out long ago, but God provided fresh water for them, from a rock, no less! A month earlier they were singing praises to God after safely crossing the Red Sea. Now they are railing against their leaders: Moses, his brother Aaron, and his sister Miriam. "Murmuring," or whining, seems way too calm to describe the anger they express. Forgotten is the harsh treatment of the slave masters and remembered is the soup pot with meat and vegetables. A little distance and new hardships sometimes make what was left behind look so much better. Yet a food crisis is no small problem. Read Exodus 16:1–30 to see what happens.

Why do you think the Israelites so quickly forgot the trials of living as Egyptian slaves?

"Those who gathered much had nothing over, and those who gathered little had no shortage; they gathered as much as each of them needed" (v. 18). No pantry here with stacks of canned goods or a freezer filled with frozen meals and ice cream bars. This "bread from heaven" was sufficient for each person, man, woman, and child. Go a little wild and gather lots and you still have only what you need. Have trouble bending over to pick it up and the little you gather will still be no more or no less than will feed you for the day. God provided their daily bread . . . every day. It made no difference if you were strong or weak, young or old, healthy or sick; God gave you what you needed.

At the same time, God had a provision regarding this food gathering so that the people could rest on the Sabbath. That provision alone should have been welcome to these slaves, for slavery has no regard for a day off. Some interpreters of this passage place the message of the sabbath above that of God as provider for the Israelites at this moment. Remember that this is before Moses received the Ten Commandments. Up to this point, only God rests on the seventh day.

One day at a time. Anyone who knows about or has been in a recovery group or twelve-step program is familiar with that phrase. Just take it one day at a time. Don't worry about tomorrow and whether you can stay away from the alcohol, the drugs, or the calorie-laden dessert. Just take care of yourself this day. God is saying to the Israelites, "Don't worry about tomorrow. I will provide what you need, not more and not less, each day. I will even make it possible that you have a day of rest and you will still have food for the day when there is no food to gather."

This daily allotment of food reminds us of a line from the prayer that Jesus taught his disciples: "Give us each day our daily bread" (Luke 11:3). Your Bible probably has a footnote at this verse, noting that it can also be translated as "bread for tomorrow," which gives the verse a reading reminiscent of the service of Communion. The Greek word can also be translated as "essential." We will, for this purpose, go with the first translation and a plain reading of that verse. God will give us, each of us, what we need each day.

Turn to Luke 11 in your Bible and look at the context for verse 3. Jesus is responding to a request about prayer from his disciples. His answer is to them as a group, not individually. Communal prayer, one that is prayed by the community or group of believers, was common at this time. The use of "us" and "we" suggests that Jesus meant this prayer to be prayed together. (His model of praying alone, noted frequently in the Gospel of Luke, suggests that we should pray individually as well.) So Jesus appears to be providing us with a petition in this prayer that reminds us to ask for our daily needs. His disciples might well have recalled the story of God's manna or bread from heaven when they heard these words.

Before we turn to these words and life today, one more interpretation is helpful. Jesus would not have been speaking Greek, of course, and probably not Hebrew. The common language of his time was Aramaic. In Aramaic, the word is *lachma*, meaning both bread and understanding. One way that Neil Douglas-Klotz translates this sentence in *Prayers of the Cosmos: Meditations on the Aramaic Words of Jesus* is "Grant what we need each day in bread and insight: subsistence for the call of growing life."[1]

A teaching about having enough for each day, the insight necessary for each day, is difficult to comprehend in an affluent society and a culture that is bulging with information. Determining what is enough for one person, one family, for this day is no small feat. First, we recognize that what is enough for the kindergarten child is not enough for her teenage brother,

either in food or in knowledge. Needs differ, but according to Exodus, each will have enough. Second, in our age of global communication, what *is* enough for us? Thinking of food alone, having our lunch "super-sized" because it is only a few pennies more may look like a smart move economically, but is it? How do we interpret "enough" in a country whose children are increasingly overweight? How many times can we sit in front of the television and watch the same scenes of children dying before we become immune to the reality of that loss of life? When is anything *enough*?

How does thinking of "us" as your family rather than "me" change this line of Jesus' prayer for you? "Us" as your community? "Us" as the world?

Take a few moments to think about just one aspect of your life. Without comparing yourself to anyone else in your neighborhood, on television, or in the news, explore how you would know the definition of enough.

What is necessary, enough for you for one day?

All of these aspects of stewardship and our role as a Christian family are about choosing deliberately to live as called by God, but that choice is not so simple. "Unless we consciously decide to live otherwise, we may drift aimlessly with the currents of daily routine rather than deliberately choose to live as part of God's kingdom."[2]

Fasting

The Bible passages we've discussed are not about fasting. However, in affluent nations simply talking about having enough for each day must surely lead us to thinking about what we have that we do not need for daily sustenance. Fasting is usually associated with giving up food for a specified time, although contemporary definitions go beyond that. Combine the general concept of fasting with the idea of abstinence and you have a spiritual practice that is almost mandatory for Christians in North America. Our tendency, though, is to compare ourselves to a neighbor (whether a few blocks away or observed in the media) who has more than we have. We rarely compare ourselves to the neighbors who have considerably less than we have, the ones we observe on television or as we drive to work.

> Where do you place your family in the economic scale of your community? in the world? Why?

Each member of the Ingram and Kim families named one thing for which she or he was thankful. They went around the table several times, each naming something else. In the discussion, the ideas of affluence and having enough were a bit confusing for Jason Ingram and David Kim. However, Melissa Ingram and Rachel Kim were more aware of children in their schools who had more and also who had less than they did. The two families continued to talk about how

they might discover what constituted "enough" for them. They recognized that because they were different in many ways, the definition of "enough" would also be different. They agreed, each member of each family, to a period of fasting until their next meeting together. At first, they thought each family would choose its own type of fast. However, as their discussion never seemed to separate into family groups, they decided that both families would begin by giving up desserts on Sunday since they often went out to eat after church. David was a little disheartened when he learned that giving up dessert at the restaurant also meant that he could not come home and eat ice cream. Nevertheless, he agreed to give it a try. At the end of the month, they would pool their "no desserts" money and choose a program to receive it.

Decisions about Lifestyle

This chapter focuses on three of many ways your family should consider how its call to stewardship can be implemented beyond your family and congregation and into the world. One way is your participation in community building, in being good neighbors. This can extend from the people who live next door to you to those on the other side of the planet. Another way is deciding how you care for and live on this planet Earth. Environmental stewardship can clearly be drawn from the creation stories in Genesis and is of great concern in these times. Yet another way is peacemaking, which is akin to community building but ranges well beyond that. As you read this section, ponder which direction your family might take at this time, knowing that you can choose another direction later.

Community Building

Look first outside your door. Which neighbor would you call if you needed a quart of milk? Which neighbor would you call if you needed help of any kind and were home alone? Living in a community, large or small, is about relationships. You don't have to be best friends with the family next door, but knowing them by name and having at least a nodding acquaintance will go a long way toward developing a community in your neighborhood, whether it is a country lane or a city street. Periodically an article appears in the newspaper about a block or neighborhood where a group has been determined to foster a sense of community with a block party or neighborhood picnic. The first attempt may not yield much. Nevertheless, concerted effort will move you in a positive direction.

Mary Ingram saw the "for sale" sign next door when she came home from work. She wasn't surprised because she knew that the family was moving due to job changes. The day the new family moved in, she invited them over for sandwiches at their convenience. When the Ingrams moved into their house, it took weeks to meet their immediate neighbors. She did not want that to happen for this family.

Unfortunately, a crisis is often what precipitates a move toward getting to know one another. After September 11, 2001, reports sprung up all over the nation of groups coming together in their neighborhoods. We realized that we needed one another if we were going to weather this tragedy and care for one another in the wake of future tragedies. The flurry has abated, but the need is ever present.

Try on some of these examples to see how they might fit your family, its call, and your particular circumstances:

—Host a simple get-together for a few families who live nearby. Include single adults and couples without children as well. If people do not know one another, provide name tags. As you write the invitation list, mix up new and old residents, both in age and time in the area.

—With another neighbor, welcome new families or residents with a picnic or potluck supper. If you enjoy games, play some that help everyone learn more about one another, not just the old neighbors getting to know the new neighbor.

—Encourage and support people you think would be good representatives on the school board or town council. Consider running for office yourself.

—Take part in civic events. Go with your family to parades and picnics sponsored by groups in your community. Look for ways to support them with your volunteer time as well.

—Join other families in your neighborhood to adopt a stretch of highway that you will keep free of trash. Working together on a project accomplishes much more than the task.

A slight digression: When my husband was diagnosed with Alzheimer's disease, a deacon from my congregation offered to recruit church members to visit him so I could continue serving on church committees, attend a support group, use my season tickets for the theater, or just have lunch or dinner with a friend. This offer came even before I realized the necessity of it. It did not take more than one or two occasions of recruiting a visitor myself, however, to realize what a gracious gift this was to me and to him. Over thirty persons visited him. People were most generous in their willingness to be with him, once they knew the need and how they could help. I was able to continue parts of my life that were important to my well-being. Had I needed to make the arrangements each time I wanted to go somewhere without him, I would soon have given up the committees, the theater ticket, and quiet visits with friends. The support group I would have managed to attend, but perhaps not every month.

I know from conversations with caregivers that few of them are as blessed as I was during that time. Most caregivers struggle to keep their heads above water, just getting the groceries and the essential tasks completed. As you think about your neigh-

borhood and your community, who could benefit from visits so that a caregiver can have a brief respite and so that the person receiving care can see a new face? Not every homebound person is ill; children can benefit from knowing such persons, and those you visit may enjoy the energy and delight of children.

Extend your gaze beyond your neighborhood. The possibilities of contributing to the community are not limited to the people you meet. Look for ways that your family might contribute to the welfare of adults and children in other places, people you will never meet. Here is a list to get you started, but your denomination will have opportunities too:

Church World Service
28606 Phillips Street
Box 968
Elkhart, Indiana 46515
info@churchworldservice.org
www.churchworldservice.org

Habitat for Humanity
121 Habitat Street
Americus, Georgia 31709
publicinfo@hfhi.org
www.habitat.org

Heifer Project International
P.O. Box 8058
Little Rock, Arkansas 72203
info@heifer.org
www.heifer.org

UNICEF
333 E. 38th Street
New York, New York 10016
information@unicefusa.org
www.unicef.org or www.unicefusa.org

> What community-building acts might your family initiate?

Communities are built as individual persons, and families, show their care by acts of mercy and attention. These acts may be large or small. They grow out of our generosity toward one another. They grow out of our call to be God's people and our knowledge that we are each, every one of us, made in God's image.

Environmental Concerns

Another way that we live out our call as God's stewards is as we participate in life together on this planet created by God. There is no shortage in options for considering how we care for the earth. The difficulty is deciding what we ought to do. Supplement the suggestions here with opportunities already existing in your area. Your participation in the community of the environment can be local, global, or both. It can be as simple as buying a live Christmas tree, planting it in your yard or a nearby park (with permission, of course), and caring for it. It can change your entire lifestyle—for example, deciding to ride a bicycle to work instead of driving your car. The physical abilities of each family member, as well as the commitment each is willing to make, will frame the way that you participate together in caring for the earth.

As the Lees and the Ingrams talked about caring for the environment, they were surprised at how eager their children were to be a part of the conversation. David told of the box for recycling paper in his kindergarten classroom. At the end of the week, they weighed the box to see how much paper they had kept out of the landfill. However, the desire to have lots of paper at the end of the week apparently motivated the children to use lots of paper so that it could go into the recycling box. David said, "Friday we took every piece of paper out of the box to make sure it was no good." Not only was recycling a virtue, now making full use of each sheet of paper gained merit too.

Many communities recycle plastic jugs, paper, aluminum cans, plastic bags, or some combination thereof. However, the first use of wood products and plastic products might be a focus for your family. Keep track of all the paper products you use in a week, from each tissue to the number of newspaper pages. Don't forget the paper towels, paper napkins, and paper plates and cups. Put all the nonrecyclable paper products that would go into your garbage in a separate trash bag. Together plan how you can use fewer nonrecyclable paper products by substituting cloth towels or napkins and nondisposable dishes. How would that change your lifestyle? What tasks would that mean for each family member?

> How might your family review its use of natural resources from the point of view that you are stewards of God's creation?

Monitor the use of the family car. Explore the availability of public transportation. Check out ways to carpool to work, to children's activities, to anywhere. Measure distances and plot safe routes for walking instead of driving.

April 22 is Earth Day. How might your family mark this day? Will you examine your call and how you are stewards of the earth? Will you participate in a project that is more global, such as the reforestation of the rainforests? Watch your local newspaper and television news broadcasts for announcements of Earth Day activities. If you discover activities too late to take part, have your own Earth Day a few days later.

Working for Peace

In a world torn apart by wars and terrorism, working for peace sounds like an impossible task, one better left to world leaders. Certainly that arena for peacemaking is vital to the interest of everyone and should be in our hearts and our prayers daily. We may find ways to affect the actions of national leaders through letters, marches, and other activities. All of that is vital, but the peacemaking for this discussion is about how we live together and how we teach our children about living together in harmony. Far too many examples of violence and the harsh treatment of persons appear on the news each day in our own communities for us to restrict the discussion of peacemaking to international affairs.

When does your child have an opportunity to get to know children different from her or him?

From those early stories of creation in Genesis, we learn that God is creator of all and correspondingly that each person is created in God's image. If nothing else, that knowledge alone demands that we treat one another with respect.

Several years ago, a wave of hate activities against Jews occurred in Billings, Montana. Ku Klux Klan fliers were left on cars; tombstones were overturned in the Jewish cemetery; a brick was thrown through the window of a home displaying a menorah. The community took immediate action. Perhaps the most effective action was a simple one. The local newspaper printed a full-page menorah in the paper and urged readers to tape it to a window in their home or business. This quiet gesture spoke volumes as the menorahs sprung up all over the community—in homes Jewish and otherwise—reinforcing the statements and proclamations of religious groups, a labor union, and numerous residents. The hate crimes stopped.

A message of hatred cannot take hold if we look at the face of the other person rather than categorize the person by ethnic identity, economic group, or impairment of ability. Children who are fortunate enough to grow up in a household that seeks to include among their friends people of all situations will surely be less likely to judge others by skin color or the sound of their speech. Think about the people who come to your home, those you invite for meals. How are these people alike and different from you?

A message of hatred cannot take hold if we have opportunities to sit and talk with groups usually labeled as different in our community. For many years, religious communities have recognized the need for Christians and Jews to talk together, with the hope that eventually they will discuss what is different about them as well as what is alike. Today, those conversations should include Muslims. We need to learn about and understand the faith of these neighbors. In the process, we may just develop a better understanding of Christianity and our own faith.

A message of hatred cannot take hold if understanding is promoted rather than fear and information rather than gossip. Derogatory names and jokes with a minority group as the brunt slip into many conversations. Your reaction in these instances is paramount to peacemaking. Each time we remain silent, the assumption is that we agree. Our silence allows the seed of hatred to send down one more root. The message we want to give our children, and the world around us, is that we will not tolerate such insensitive behavior.

Another place for peacemaking may come a little closer to home. Bullying, at any age and for any reason, should not be acceptable for your family. Bullying might be identified at its worse in hate crimes, but bullying cuts across age lines and is found from a young age on. Expecting children to work out difficulties when the power is uneven and when no adults are giving adequate support is setting children up to fail. Working for peace may mean promoting a no-tolerance-for-bullies policy in the school or other organizations for children.

As your family looks at the possibilities for peacemaking together,

pray that God will guide your decision making.

How are your children learning about faiths other than Christianity?

A Prayer for Our Stewardship throughout the World

Leader: God of all creation and giver of all that we need, give us caring hearts to build communities of trust wherever we live.

Response: Send us your Spirit, Holy God.

Leader: God of all creation and giver of all that we need, give us caring hands to tend to your creation, every part of it.

Response: Send us your Spirit, Holy God.

Leader: God of all creation and giver of all that we need, give us caring minds to seek peace in our families, our communities, and around the world.

Response: Send us your Spirit, Holy God. Amen.

Summary

In Mark 3:31–35, Jesus reconfigures our relationship to our family. While we will always be important to one another as family members, our center or locus is not our family unit but God. This is what it means to be called

What from this discussion about stewardship in the community, near or worldwide, will be included in your "family rule"?

by God. This is what it means to order our life together as God's stewards. Not only do we care for one another because we are related in some manner, but we extend that care to others outside our family, to our immediate community or neighborhood and farther into the world. What we are finally able to do is important, but more important is our recognition of one another as children of God and our concern for the welfare of one another.

Seeking a Release from Too Much Stuff

The spiritual practice of fasting can be traced to the Hebrew Scriptures, when the Israelites were urged to fast as a way to confess corporately before God. Jesus fasted and prayed in the wilderness before beginning his ministry. Fasting spiritually, according to John Calvin, is also a means of cleansing oneself of needless desires. This is, perhaps, the kind of fasting that Christians in North America ought to explore in the twenty-first century.

The question to ask when examining your life, individually or as a family, in preparation for fasting is "What do I have or do that prevents me from recognizing God's gifts?" Here is a list of potential areas to examine:

—Work—Does your work so rule your life that it diminishes your family life? Why do you work as hard as you do?

—Food—How much food is stored in your home right now? How much food is thrown away in your house on a daily basis? How many times a day do you eat . . . anything?

—Exercise—Do you exercise to keep your body fit, or has exercising become a mania that dominates your week?

—Shopping—How often do you shop when you have no need to buy something? How do ads influence what you do purchase?

—Things—What in your closet or in your home has not been used in the past year?

—Computer—How many hours do you spend checking e-mail, instant messaging, or playing games on your computer each week?

—(Fill in your own area and appropriate question)

1. When fasting as a family, select one thing that you will do without, such as television on Friday nights, dessert on Saturdays, or computer games on Sundays. Look for something that your family can truly give up together.

2. Decide how long (months, weeks) you will do without this thing. Choose a good length of time so that you actually experience life without it. However, don't set such a long time at the beginning that the idea alone sends everyone into a state of depression.

3. Select something to substitute for the time you have given up or something to benefit from the money you will save. For example, instead of watching television on Friday nights, invite another family over for games—the practice of hospitality. Instead of having dessert on Saturday, place the money the dessert would have cost in a jar on the dining table and give the money to a hunger-prevention program—practicing generosity through giving. Many people who fast on a regular basis replace mealtimes with times for prayer and meditation. How might your family add prayer or some other spiritual practice in place of the thing you have given up?

Chapter 5
Just Do It!

Our desire to be good stewards of all that God has given not only allows us to serve but also compels us to seek justice for God's creation. Seeking justice begins at an early age as children discover the words "fair" and "not fair." First, those words are about what is happening to them. Later, they see injustice in what is happening to their peers. Parents help their children continue to grow as they join them in exploring justice issues beyond themselves and their peer groups. As we serve persons in our community and come up against injustices, we know that the church is called to right these wrongs. We hear that call in the prophets' words to the nation of Israel. It also comes to us as it did to the early church through the stories about and teachings of Jesus.

Amos 5:14–15, 21–24 and Luke 18:1–8

Amos was a prophet, but he didn't start out as one. Amos was a shepherd when God sent him with a message of social justice for Israel, the northern kingdom. The book of Amos is a series of short speeches, describing his visions from God and giving the people God's message. It reads like much Hebrew poetry, where the second line echoes the message of the first line. Read Amos 5:14–15 and 21–24.

The message Amos had for Israel centered on the establishment of justice for all. This justice was to be founded on the practice of good by the people. Then, maybe Yahweh would show mercy to the last remnant of the chosen people. Certainly, they would not be able to fool Yahweh with their pious worship or great show of generosity. No, what Yahweh wants to see is righteousness and justice so bountiful that they come cascading over everything and everyone.

> How might you present Amos's words in contemporary language and for the church today?

Now, turn to the Christian Scriptures and read Luke 18:1–8. This widow is calling for justice too, but it certainly isn't cascading down from anywhere. In a commentary on this gospel, Fred Craddock repeats the interpretation of an elderly black minister after reading this story: "Until you have stood for years knocking at a locked door, your knuckles bleeding, you do not really know what prayer is."[1] While Jesus tells this story to teach about praying, it is but a short

> What contemporary figures (female or male) remind you of the persistent widow?

step to connect it to the struggle to seek justice. In working for justice and righteousness, our prayer becomes our work, and our work, our prayer. If not, we soon become weary and leave the work to others.

Seeking Justice

It is not by chance that the spiritual practice of advocacy, or seeking justice, comes in the last chapter. This practice builds on generosity and compassion, which we know begins to develop in young children. Seeking justice requires a sense of fairness as well to push us beyond the boundary of our own lives to enter the lives and needs of others so strongly that we are willing to stand with and for them.

Advocacy Settings

Seeking justice requires us to step into new territory, into the land of the other. For most people this is not comfortable. The mother in chapter 3 who served the evening meal in the shelter confessed as much when she reported on her experience for her church newsletter. She acknowledged that even the thought of being in the presence of strangers, much less strangers in these circumstances, sent her fleeing. She looked back on the evening with wonder at the way everyone took whatever happened in stride . . . even when preparing the meal took longer than she expected.

Perhaps the step into the new territory was not so big for that family, but for others who show us the way, it is. In the nineteenth century, Father Damian, a Roman Catholic priest in the Hawaiian Islands, stepped into the world of people with leprosy when they were cast aside and there was no cure for the disease. He requested this assignment in order to live among them and minister to them; eventually, he died from leprosy.

Elizabeth Fry, also in the nineteenth century, was asked to go to Newgate Prison to see the dreadful conditions. Appalled at the crowding as well as the lack of bedding and warm clothes, she and her sister-in-law returned the next day with blankets and clothing. Advised by the guard that it was not safe for women to go in, they went in anyway. This visit began a ministry that lasted for many years. She even testified on behalf of the prisoners before a committee of the House of Commons, the first woman ever to do so.

More recently (1982), the Rev. John Fife, a Presbyterian pastor in Tucson, Arizona, took that step when a family from El Salvador came to his church looking for help. Believing that the family and many others faced persecution if they returned to El Salvador, Fife and Jim Corbett founded the Sanctuary Movement. They, with the help of many others, provided safety for the Salvadorans. Many more stories of stepping into new territory could be told.

Few of us are called to make such big steps, but we are all called to advocate for those who are powerless. It is a natural extension of our call to be God's stewards. The few sugges-

tions that follow can begin you on a road where the steps you take will be toward new forms of justice and righteousness for God's people and God's creation.

> What is your dream for your community? Your nation? The world?

In Your Congregation

Look around your congregation on Sunday morning and at other times. Who is missing? Why are they missing? Who lacks the presence and the power to speak out for themselves? Perhaps one of these suggestions will fit what you observe:

—Advocate for the participation of homebound members in the life of your congregation. In this age, when communication and transportation is so available, no member ought to be isolated from the congregation. Find out how your congregation ministers to homebound members and how they are helped to minister to others. Not all homebound members are ill and not all are elderly. Look over these ideas to see what is not happening in your congregation and how you might advocate for change: make regular visits to the same persons so you can become friends and advocates for them; ask members to make phone calls to homebound members on a regular schedule; record the worship service and special services, such as Christmas Eve or Ash Wednesday; invite homebound members to make phone calls to the elderly to check in with them daily; look for tasks homebound members can do at home, such as stuffing mailings for the annual stewardship campaign or sending birthday cards to children in the church school.

—Advocate for members with physical handicaps to help ensure your church building is accessible to them. Most denominations have information about changes to make in public buildings so they are accessible to everyone. Get this information and take a tour of your church building. List all the areas that are not accessible. Meet with the property committee or your pastor to see what can be done to make the building more accessible for everyone.

—Advocate for the inclusion of young people in the governance of the congregation, particularly after they have joined the church. Here are a few ways that congregations have included young people: appointed them to committees, such as the youth ministry committee or the pastor search committee; included them as worship leaders (and not just on Youth Sunday); invited them to participate in service activities generally publicized for adults, activities both for the congregation and beyond.

In Your Community

Communities have many similarities, yet each is different. Get to know your community and its political structure. As you serve in ministries to people in your community, look beyond the acts of mercy to see where those being served are kept from justice by existing laws or government procedures. Perhaps these examples will open your eyes to changes that are needed where you live:

—Advocate for parents who are unemployed. Where can they go for assistance with rent and utilities? How do their children get the necessary school supplies? What job training is available? Where is affordable child care available when jobs are found?

—Advocate for older citizens on limited incomes. How do they pay for medical prescriptions? How do they get to doctor's appointments or to church if they no longer drive?

—Advocate for good schools for all children and young people. Volunteer in an after-school program to learn about the needs of children in a school in your area or a neighboring community. Find out what groups already exist that work for better education, particularly in neighborhoods where the tax base is small.

If you choose an advocacy project in your community, look for regional or national organizations with similar goals. For example, if you are advocating for children or families in poverty, check out the Web site for the Children's Defense Fund, www.childrensdefense.org. Groups and people already working in your area of concern will be able to steer you to other organizations.

In the World

Seeking justice is no longer restricted to the communities in which we live. Information about injustices around the globe is readily available on the Internet. Check for information about groups working globally from your denomination too. Here are a few Web sites to get you started:

- —Advocate for safe working conditions and for laws that put children in school, not the factory. For one specific to the manufacture of carpets, see the Web site www.rugmark.org, where you will find an action guide, "Ten Ways You Can Help End Child Labor."
- —Advocate for children around the world in various kinds of tragic circumstances by going to the Web site www.unicefusa.org and clicking on "advocacy center." There you will find links to information and action suggestions regarding children's rights, child labor, child soldiers, and landmines.
- —Advocate for peaceful resolutions to conflict rather than war. On any given day, war condi-

tions exist in many more places in the world than is reported in the daily newspaper. The Web site www.nonviolence.org provides links to a number of United States–based peace organizations as well as a list of international organizations and resources.
- —Have another interest? Check it out by searching the Internet or finding out whether your denomination is working on the same issue.

How to Keep Going

Advocacy work is hard; seeking justice takes perseverance. Gains are made slowly and sometimes not for decades. Yet we learn from the widow in Jesus' story that we do not give up. How, then, do we keep our spirits and souls ready to stay at it? Here are a few ideas, especially for families:

- —Pray to keep your spiritual resources alive. Pray as a family before and after you act to seek justice. Pray for the people who are treated unjustly in your daily prayers. Pray without ceasing.
- —Join a community of support beyond your family. Especially look for others who appreciate your commitment as a family. Get to know some of these people beyond the advocacy work.
- —As a family, read and talk about the Bible on a regular basis. This will keep your focus on God as the reason for seeking justice.

As you read and reflect on God's Word, do so as German theologian Karl Barth said: "with the Bible in one hand and the newspaper in the other." When we bring our concerns for the world to our Bible study, we connect the world and the Bible immediately. Watch the news together especially with older children and adolescents so that you can discuss the injustices reported and talk about where others are acting as advocates.

—Worship with your congregation. Your source of renewal comes from the community of faith. Don't neglect these ties as you become involved in advocacy.

—Plan Sabbath times together for renewal of your energy. Take a break from the advocacy work from time to time. Stay in touch with what is happening, but plan a Sabbath time so that you can return to your work refreshed.

A Litany for Seeking God's Justice and Righteousness

Leader: God of Righteousness, give us the wide eyes to see the lack of justice around us.

Response: Turn us from ourselves, Holy God.

Leader: God of Righteousness, give us energetic bodies to work for justice for others.

Response: Turn us from ourselves, Holy God.

Leader: God of Righteousness, give us persevering hearts to seek justice when the way is difficult.

Response: Turn us from ourselves, Holy God, and toward others so that we might find you in them. Amen.

Stewardship and Spiritual Practices

The spiritual practice of seeking justice is closely connected to the other spiritual practices in this book. Generosity plays an important role in advocacy. Giving financially is as much a part of seeking justice as is giving of your time. Hospitality may be what led you to the cause you have selected in the first place. Advocacy is about putting others first and being willing to stand with them, not over them. It is about being hospitable to those who do not agree with the stand you have taken, which is perhaps the biggest test of anyone's hospitality.

You saw how discernment plays an important role in decision making before one begins as an advocate. It continues to be an important spiritual practice along the way. Depending on the type of justice being sought, fasting can sharpen our understanding of those with whom we stand.

Summary

According to Kristine A. Haig, "stewardship is a daily discipline involving the everyday self-offering of our lives."[2] As you have read, pondered, discussed, experimented, and made decisions about the call that you and your family have from God, you have determined ways that you are to live as stewards of God's creation. Your life of stewardship continues long

As you review your "family rule," what will you add about seeking justice?

after you finish reading this book. May God's Spirit guide you as you live each day.

Be an Advocate

—Select an issue for which your family has some passion. The issue ide-ally relates to a way you have been in service so that you have seen the need firsthand.
—Spend time in prayer together deciding whether this is the issue to which your family is called.
—Talk with others who are already working for justice in this area. Find out about the options available to you, particularly those that will include your children.
—Take time to discern what direction might be the best for your family as it seeks justice through advocacy. (See page 13 for steps of dis-cernment.) Advocacy can range from prayer, to letter writing, to tes-tifying before government agencies, to picketing. Look for the combination that will best allow your entire family to participate.
— Just do it!
—Seek support from others working in the same cause and others inter-ested in it through prayer and conversation.
—Stay grounded in the life of your congregation, especially its worship life.
—After a time, take a break to talk together about what you are doing, why you are doing it, and what you hope to accomplish. Remember the story of the persistent widow . . . change may be a long time com-ing.

LEADER'S
GUIDE

Introduction

Whether you are leading all five sessions, you are one of several people taking turns at leading a session, or you just thought you would see what was here, welcome. To lead these sessions for adults or families, you need not be an expert in stewardship planning or hold an advanced degree of any sort. Each session follows the same plan:

—Opening moments
—Personal experience that connects with the focus
—Bible stories
—Connection between the Bible stories and the focus
—Working on the focus
—Closing moments

As you plan each session, take advantage of any experience or expertise the group of participants offers. Including others in leadership, from praying during the Opening Moments to reporting for a small group, gives them a greater stake in what happens during and between sessions.

For this kind of study, homework is essential. The participants are not expected to read the chapter in advance, but they will need to read it after the session and try out suggestions. Talking about being good stewards without practicing it is like talking about riding a bicycle but never getting onto that bicycle seat. As a leader, you will want to try out suggestions too. The exception to this is the retreat setting. However, even there you should encourage participants to regularly connect their discussions with their lives at home.

That brings us to a further explanation about the arrangement of the sessions that follow. You will find suggestions for adapting each session to a group of families and for a retreat setting. The basic session is designed for groups of adults. However, should you wish to have families talk about stewardship together, the ideas under "For groups of families" give additional activities. In this case, it is assumed that the children are at least eight years old. You might take a look at these activities even if your group consists only of adults.

The suggestions to adapt the sessions for retreat settings were also written with the assumption that children are present. Because there is little time to put ideas into practice during a retreat, the recommendation to keep a journal in which family members list decisions and plans is important. Otherwise, the work done at the retreat will not enter the lives of the participants once they have returned to their homes.

If you have not done so already, read the entire book before you lead the first session. Then you will have a better idea of where you are headed, and articles and news reports will grab you that you might not have otherwise

noticed. Make current stories and information part of the study too.

Planning for the Attendance of Parents

If you really want parents to come to this study, provide child care. Even if children over eight are included in the study, those families with other children under eight will need this help.

Before you set the dates, call a few families that you think would be interested and check out the dates with them. If possible, get a commitment from these families to be a part of the study. Encourage them to "talk it up" with their friends. Announcements and print publicity is important, but nothing guarantees success like an invitation from a friend.

If children will be part of the group:

—Keep the time in group discussion brief. Make more use of conversations in families and of art and drama activities.

—Provide a quiet activity corner in the room where the plenary sessions take place. In it, place modeling dough, books, drawing materials, jigsaw puzzles, and other things children can play with quietly. Let children know they can go there at any time during the sessions.

—Provide a children's library of books suggested in the bibliography at the end of the chapter and others that speak of generosity, giving, serving, and other topics from this study. Encourage children and families to check out the books to read at home, at bedtime, or during the retreat itself.

—If adults without children are present, encourage them to get to know the children and to give parents a break now and again by doing something with one or two children.

If you are not used to leading a study group:

—Be prepared. Have the supplies you need ready before anyone arrives.

—Draw on the experience of others. If you have little experience leading group discussions, talk with someone who does this regularly and ask for pointers.

—Share the leadership. Ask others to read or tell the Bible story or to lead a discussion. The participants have the same material you do, so they too can give a hand.

—Expect the participants to do the homework, but then make contingency plans for those who just don't get to it. Don't plan an activity critical to the session that depends on everyone having read the previous chapter. Even those who have may need a refresher to recall what they read.

—Relax and enjoy the study. No one expects you to be an expert. As leader, you will learn far more than anyone else anyway.

Session 1
Getting Started

Focus Question: What is God's call to our family?

Before You Begin

—If you expect participants who are not familiar with the Bible, place bookmarks in Bibles at Joshua 24 and Mark 10.

—Set out name tags and markers.

—Print the definition of stewardship from chapter 1 on newsprint or poster board: *Stewardship is how we use our resources—time, talent, and finances—to respond to God's love.*

—Prepare the reading assignment papers for Bible Stories.

Opening Moments

Materials: name tags, markers, and newsprint or poster board with the definition of stewardship

Invite the participants (all ages) to make name tags as they arrive. When everyone is settled, begin the session with this prayer or one of your own:

Holy God, thank you for bringing us here. Give us minds to dream new thoughts and hearts to hear your Word and the words of others. In Jesus' name, we pray. Amen.

Welcome the group and invite each person to tell his or her name, family configuration, and one reason he or she came to this study. If the group is larger than twelve, form groups of no more than six for these introductions. So you will know why people attend, ask one person in each group to keep a list of the reasons given by the participants.

Introduce this study by distributing copies of this book. Say a bit about stewardship, referring to the definition you displayed. Explain that for this session, the focus is on how each family understands its call from God and what that means for the family members and their life together. If you wish, describe the general format that each session will take.

For groups of families

Materials: same as previous

Have each family introduce itself as a unit. The members might create a cheer for their family that includes naming each family member.

As you introduce the study, be clear that children are important members of each family group and decision.

For a retreat setting

Materials: same as previous, felt for banners (contrasting colors for handprints), sharp scissors, white glue

Select from the previous activities as best fits the composition of the group. If you have more time for introductions, have each family begin a family banner from felt. Family members

can add to their banner handprints cut from felt.

Personal Experience of the Focus

Materials: writing paper, pencils or pens

Distribute writing paper and pencils or pens to the participants. Have them write down one decision they made in the past year that they see as a stewardship decision. If they appear stumped, remind them of the definition of stewardship used in this study. When everyone is ready, ask the group members to name the areas in which their decisions were made, such as budget, work, volunteer activity, or employment. Remind them to name the area but not describe the choice. Describing the choice would take too much time and might lead the discussion in a direction that's too personal. Ask them to keep the papers to refer to later.

For groups of families or in retreat settings

Materials: same as previous

Each family talks about decisions and reports by naming one area. The important aspect here is the family discussion, not the reporting.

Bible Stories

Materials: Bibles, assignments for the readers, newsprint, markers

Distribute the Bibles and have everyone turn to Joshua 24. Explain that Joshua 24:1–28 will be used as readers' theater. Three individual readers are needed: the narrator, the message from God, and Joshua. The rest of the group will be the Israelites. Give papers with the assignments to the volunteer readers and post the verses for the Israelites on newsprint: Narrator: 1–2a, 14a, 16a, 25–27a, 28; Message from God: 2b–13; Joshua: 14b–15, 19b, 23b, 27b; Israelites: 16b, 21b, 22c, 24b. Alternatively, photocopy the passage and highlight the part for each reader. Discuss the story with the first question in the sidebar on page 7 in chapter 1.

Then introduce the reading from Mark with the note that this story from the Gospels has a much different ending. Follow the directions in chapter 1 for reading and discussing this story.

After the readings, invite the group to compare the two stories by asking:

—What fundamental differences do you see in the decisions by Joshua and the Israelites and the young man?
—What might be a motto for the decision of the Israelites? Of the young man?
—How was each decision a stewardship decision?

For groups of families

Materials: Bible, Bible storybooks or a storyteller

If the children are mostly elementary age, read the stories from a children's Bible storybook, such as *The Family*

Story Bible (Louisville, Ky.: Westminster John Knox Press, 1996), with "The Hebrews Remember" (p. 96), and *The Children's Bible in 365 Stories* (Oxford, England: Lion Publishing Corp., 1985), with "The Man with a Lot of Money" (p. 331). Or invite a storyteller to tell the Bible stories at each session. In the Joshua story, provide speaking parts for the Israelites that children and adults can read together.

For a retreat setting

Materials: Bible

Engage a storyteller for the retreat, who will tell each of the Bible stories to the group. During the discussion, provide Bibles for readers to use.

The Focus and the Bible Stories

To think beyond the storyline, ask the group: How did Joshua and the Israelites determine how they would respond to God?

In the same way, center their attention on the story from Mark with this question: How did the young man in Mark's story determine his mission?

Move from the stories to consideration of the process that might have led to the decision in each story. Note that the thought of each is not available to us. However, over the centuries, Christians have developed a spiritual practice of discernment to help them make important faith decisions.

So that everyone has a chance to speak, have each person or couple find a partner person or couple (or arrange them in advance) and discuss the stories in this smaller group.

Conclude this activity by reading or saying in your own words the description of discernment on page 13. Invite questions for clarification.

For groups of families

Assign each family one of the Bible stories and give them this question: How did the man or the Israelites come to their decision? After time for their discussion, pair up families who had different stories to exchange the conclusions from their individual discussions.

For a retreat setting

In small groups, role-play an Israelite household discussing the question from Joshua. Bring everyone together to hear what issues arose during the discussions. Then have the group discuss the man's decision in the story from Mark.

Working with the Focus

Materials: copies of this book, newsprint, markers

Have the group turn to "Coming to an Important Decision Together" (p. 13) in their books. Go over the steps for discernment there. Have the group brainstorm ideas to question 1. Record the ideas on newsprint. Be clear that this is a question for each family but that brainstorming ideas will get them ready to do this as parents. Stop the brainstorming while the ideas are still flowing.

Turn now to the idea of a family "rule." Describe a rule as it is used in community, using the description on page 10. Then look together at those from Judith Smith (p. 10). If there is time, talk together about the kind of "rule" that might be workable and appropriate for the participating families by looking at the areas on page 11.

When it is almost time to close, ask the group to do these things before the next session:

—Read chapter 1.
—Write a family statement in response to God's call to them.
—Talk about a potential "rule" for their family.
—Bring their books to the next session.

For groups of families

Materials: copies of this book, newsprint or writing paper, markers or pens

Begin the process of discernment rather than talk about it. Point out "Coming to an Important Decision Together" (p. 13). Each family might get through the third step. They can continue the discernment at home. Allow time for each family to report at the next session.

For a retreat setting

Materials: newsprint and markers, family banners, fabric paint

When a family has discerned its mission phrase or statement, a family member can print it on the banner with fabric paint.

Have parents or family groups complete the discernment process and begin developing a family "rule."

Closing Moments

Materials: copies of this book

Prayer together the litany on page 9.

You or a participant can read the Leader lines.

Leader Evaluation

What ideas need reinforcement or expansion in the next session? If new participants arrive, how will you incorporate them? How did each participant connect with the focus?

Session 2
At Home

Focus Question: How do we make faithful use
of family time together?

Before You Begin

—Place bookmarks in the Bibles at Exodus 18 and Luke 10.
—Prepare a newsprint sheet for each family unit. Divide it into blocks corresponding to the church year and add the dates of the Sundays. Begin the dates with a Sunday in a couple weeks.

Opening Moments

Materials: name tags (optional)

Welcome the group and pray this prayer or one of your own:

> Welcoming God, we return to this group, ready to discover more about the ways we might use our resources to reflect our gratitude for your love. In the name of Jesus, we pray. Amen.

Request any reports on ideas, activities, or questions from the previous session. Perhaps some participants will report on the family mission statement they created. Others may have a question or comment from reading chapter 1. Through these reports, help the group review what happened in the first session. Add any comments you wish to make that review complete.

Present the focus for this session (family life as a setting for stewardship decisions) and this session's focus question.

For groups of families

Materials: poster board, markers, masking tape, ink pad, and paper towels (optional)

Invite comments from the participants on completing the discernment of their family mission statement at home. As a review, have each family create a simple poster with its mission statement. Each family member can sign or put a thumbprint on the poster.

For a retreat setting

Materials: banners from Session 1

Have each family walk around the space carrying its banner.

Personal Experience of the Focus

Materials: newsprint, markers

Give each person or family unit a large sheet of newsprint and a marker. On it they are to list the birthdays and anniversaries of family members. For now, keep this to the immediate family unit. Then have them add any significant dates that will occur in the next twelve months, such as a graduation or special anniversary.

Bible Stories

Materials: Bibles

Introduce the Exodus story with the information in chapter 2. Then invite two men to read the conversation between Moses and Jethro. Discuss the questions about the story on page 16 in chapter 2.

Follow a similar process with Luke 10:38–42. This time, ask for volunteers to portray Jesus, Mary, and Martha, reading their parts in the text. Discuss the questions about this story that are on page 16 of chapter 2.

For groups of families

Materials: children's Bible storybook or a storyteller

Include the children in the Exodus story by having them line up to have questions answered or arguments settled by Moses.

Both stories can be told by a storyteller (if you have chosen to present the stories in that way). The Exodus story of Moses and Jethro is hard to find in children's Bible storybooks, but the story of Mary and Martha is readily available.

For a retreat setting

Materials: simple costumes for all ages

Recruit people to act out both Bible stories rather than reading the text. Children can line up as Israelites as described earlier.

The Focus and the Bible Stories

Materials: copies of this book

To encourage the participants to bring the two Bible stories together, ask these questions:

—In the two stories, what was the "family time" difficulty?
—In the two stories, what was the "family tasks" difficulty?
—What about these stories is important for families to think about today?

During the discussion of the last question, introduce hospitality as an important spiritual practice for families at home. Read "The Practice of Hospitality and Family Time" (p. 25). Invite their comments and ideas about how they already practice hospitality in any of the ways suggested.

For groups of families

Materials: copies of this book

Discuss the first two questions under "Focus and the Bible Stories" in plenary. Then in family units, have them talk about the third question. Return to the plenary to introduce hospitality as a spiritual practice.

For a retreat setting

Materials: copies of this book

Consider the previous plan for groups of families as well. After introducing the spiritual practice of hospitality, have each family unit dramatize an act

of hospitality for the other participants to identify, like a game of charades.

Working with the Focus

Materials: newsprint, markers (at least two different colors for each family unit), copies of this book

To each family unit, distribute the newsprint with the church year that you prepared in advance along with markers of two different colors. Explain the church year if people are not familiar with it, referring to the information in chapter 2.

Have each family unit add the birthdays, anniversaries, and other special occasions from the list they created at the beginning of the session. When everyone has finished, explain that they are going to look specifically at opportunities to build family time into the celebration of special occasions, whether family based or church year based. Refer them to "The Church Year and the Stewardship of Family Time" (p. 18). Suggest that they work on steps 3 and 4 in the process described there.

When it is almost time to conclude the session, bring everyone together and ask the participants to do these things before the next session:

—Read chapter 2.
—Complete the family time portion of the church year chart. Talk about "More than the Time Together" and "The Family as

Conserver of Family Stories" in chapter 2.

—Write down anything that grows out of this session that would be a part of their "family rule."

For groups of families

Materials: copies of this book, church year chart, poster board and markers (or jars and materials to decorate them)

Begin with the development of the church year calendar by having each family unit add birthdays, anniversaries, and special occasions. Rather than having them work on it, which they can do at home, move to the ideas for assigning family tasks (p. 20). Provide poster board for chart making and jars or containers for those families who decide to have a drawing to determine tasks.

For a retreat setting

Materials: copies of this book, church year charts, markers (at least two different colors in quantity), poster board, jars and materials to decorate them, scrapbook pages or construction paper, three-ring binders, assorted art materials

Set up centers (with the directions that follow) for all three areas of family life stewardship: family time, family tasks, and family stories. Be available to clarify directions and help, but encourage the families to move through the centers at their own pace.

—Family time: Read "The Church Year and the Stewardship of Family Time" in chapter 2. Follow the directions there to create a church year chart and make preliminary decisions about events you will celebrate in the next two months. If they are events you normally celebrate, what might you add to that celebration?

—Family tasks: Read "More than Time Together" in chapter 2. Decide whether your family would prefer a chart or a jar to assign family tasks. Then make the chart or decorate a jar.

—Family stories: Read "The Family as Conserver of Family Stories" in chapter 2. Begin a scrapbook of family memories. Design the first page to introduce your family members. Then begin to collect family stories to add to your scrapbook. Invite a scrapbook enthusiast to be a consultant for this center.

Closing Moments

Materials: copies of this book

Pray together the litany on page 22. Form two groups, one to read the Leader part and the other to read the Response.

For groups of families

Materials: copies of this book

Invite a family to read the Leader part.

For a retreat setting
Bring everyone together and talk about what they did. Perhaps each family can tell a family story at a campfire later.

Leader Evaluation

A lot happened in this session; how might you encourage the participants to do what they can and set other ideas aside until later? What ideas seemed to garner the most interest?

Session 3
At Church

Focus Question: How can our family develop generous habits of giving and serving?

Before You Begin

—Place bookmarks in the Bibles at Deuteronomy 15 and John 12.
—Prepare eight sheets of newsprint, one with each point in "Ways to Nurture Generosity" in chapter 3. It is not necessary to include the question with each point.
—Make copies of the case study you select for Working with the Focus.

Opening Moments

Welcome the group and pray this prayer or one of your own:

Generous God, we gather again to discover more about being faithful stewards of all that you provide for us. Open our hearts and hands to your will. In Jesus' name, we pray. Amen.

Invite participants to report on their family activities related to choosing family time and family tasks. Then suggest that they report on how they have chosen to share family stories. Finally, seek any comments or questions on chapter 2. Add any comments you wish to complete this review of the previous session and chapter 2.

Present the focus question for this session. Note how it connects with the work from the previous session about stewardship at home, basing your comments on the opening of chapter 3.

For groups of families

Materials: family posters, markers

Invite a family unit to read the opening prayer in unison.

Suggest that each family add something to its poster to indicate the choices made based on chapter 2. Display the posters for everyone to see.

For a retreat setting

Materials: family banners, felt, scissors, white glue, fabric paint

Because the sessions come closer together in a retreat, the review need not be extensive. Each family unit can add something to its banner that suggests a choice to try at home.

Personal Experience of the Focus

Working alone, ask the participants to recall a time when their family, themselves included, served someone else or a time when their family unit did that more recently. After time to remember such an occasion, have each person find a partner and tell his or her stories to each other.

For groups of families

Have each family recall such a time and pantomime it for the rest of the group to identify. If there are more than eight families, form small groups to do this.

For a retreat setting

Ask each family to recall such a time and prepare to dramatize it in a brief skit of no more than two minutes.

Bible Stories

Materials: Bibles

Provide Bibles for any participants without them. Read the first two paragraphs under "Deuteronomy 15:7–11 and John 12:1–8" in chapter 3 to the group. Then proceed to read and discuss the Deuteronomy and John passages as suggested in chapter 3. Include the questions on page 28 during the discussion.

For groups of families

While the Deuteronomy passage is not a story, it can be presented in a story framework. For example, the storyteller may begin by reminding the group of the Exodus and the difficulties the Israelites faced as slaves in Egypt. Then involve the participants in recalling the Exodus story from session 2 and note how the people were thankful for God's deliverance from Egypt—so thankful that they performed acts of generosity to others. These words from Deuteronomy remind them of their response to God's generosity.

The story from John needs no adaptation and can be found in many children's Bible storybooks.

For a retreat setting

Suggest to the storyteller the adaptation of Deuteronomy from "For groups of families." If possible, move to a different site for each story—a physical way of pointing to the amount of time that elapsed between the Deuteronomy passage and the story from John's Gospel.

The Focus and the Bible Stories

Materials: newsprint, markers, masking tape

Follow the discussion of the Bible with a discussion of generosity. Begin with the question on page 28 in chapter 3. Encourage the participants to describe their own experiences of generosity, whether as giver or recipient. Then turn to "Ways to Nurture Generosity" (p. 36) in chapter 3. If possible, form eight small groups (anywhere from two to five people each) and assign each one a numbered statement and question from the list. Have them read and discuss the statement so that all are clear about the meaning. Then ask them to quickly list four or five answers to the question that they will report to the whole group.

During the report time, have the group read its statement in unison. One or two group members can report their answers to the question.

For groups of families

Materials: newsprint, markers, masking tape

Focus on the fourth and fifth steps in the list of ways to nurture generosity (p. 36). Put two family units together.

Half of these smaller groups will brainstorm answers to question 4 and the others, question 5. If you have more than one smaller group discussing a question, combine their lists for the same question as you write them on newsprint.

For a retreat setting

Materials: newsprint, markers, crayons, masking tape

Select the statements and questions from "Ways to Nurture Generosity" (p. 36) that you want to highlight. For example, if your group includes adults without children in their homes, they might examine question 2 and think of ways that your congregation might be more aware of and involved with the children of the congregation. Parents of very young children might gather to explore answers to question 8. Sort the participants as you have planned. Then have the various groups list their ideas on newsprint. The children can add decorations and illustrations to the newsprint. Post them for everyone to read and at an eye level comfortable for everyone, especially the children.

Working with the Focus

Materials: copies of the case study you selected

You will not have time to examine all three areas that are highlighted: when the congregation gathers, when the congregation serves, and when the congregation gives. Select the one that you think will be of most interest to the participants. Read that section aloud or have the participants read it silently. Then open the discussion with a request for comments or questions for clarification.

Select the case study from page 79 for the area you have chosen. Distribute copies of it and ask a volunteer to read it aloud. Then invite the group to talk about ways that family might proceed. Follow the discussion of the case study with the questions at the end of the appropriate section in chapter 3.

Conclude this part of the session with the following assignments before the next session:

—Read chapter 3.
—At a family meeting, read and discuss "When the Congregation Gives."
—Plan one activity each for gather, serve, and give as it relates to your congregation.
—Consider an addition to your "family rule" based on generosity.

For groups of families

Materials: copies of this book, newsprint, markers

Have each family prepare the calendar for the previous four weeks. Then have them add to it the times when they gather with the congregation and the times when they serve with the congregation. Each family can read the sections in chapter 3 for a clearer understanding of the two times. When they finish, ask them to compare their calendar to the answers they gave or heard in the discussion of generosity earlier.

For a retreat setting

Materials: copies of this book, poster board, markers

Form three groups. Assign one category (gather, serve, give) to each group. They are to read that section of chapter 3 and prepare an ad to promote that aspect of stewardship and congregational life. The ad can be a skit or a print ad on poster board.

Closing Moments

Materials: copies of this book

Conclude with "A Prayer for Our Stewardship at Church" (p. 34). Have part of the group read the Leader lines and the rest of the group read the Response.

Leader Evaluation

Judging from the conversation, what additional resources do the participants need in order to act on the suggestions in this chapter? Print resources? People resources? What ideas came from the group that might be reported to the church staff or particular committees of the congregation?

Case Studies

When the Congregation Gathers

As the Ingram family looked over the chart they had made with the times that they gathered with their congregation, it didn't take long to see that rarely was the family in the same place with all generations of the congregation. On Sunday morning, they were in age groupings. Mary and John usually chose to attend worship when the children were in church school. They hadn't even stayed for the fellowship hour in the four weeks on the chart.

What conversation might follow this examination of the chart?

When the Congregation Serves

Lee Kim and his children had just finished adding the ways that they served others through their congregation. They noted that together they shopped for canned food for the food pantry each month. During the month they also gave up desserts on Sunday and had given the money saved to the hunger offering of the congregation. Before Lee could say a word, David piped up, "Who gets this food and who spends this money, anyway?"

What conversation might follow David's question?

When the Congregation Gives

Mary Ingram was still thinking about her childhood and the avoidance of conversation about money. John, who had not grown up in the church, was having a hard time figuring out what it meant to be good stewards of their finances. At the dinner table, Mary asked Melissa if any of her friends got allowances.

What conversation might follow Melissa's answer?

Session 4
In the Community

*Focus Question: How is our family God's steward
in the community of the world?*

Before You Begin

—Place bookmarks at Exodus 16
and Luke 11 in the Bibles.

—Gather children's books pertinent to the three areas: community building, environmental
concerns, and peacemaking. See
suggestions in the bibliography
(p. 95) and talk with a children's
librarian or teacher of young
children for other ideas. Display
the books for the participants to
look at. Children's books are a
good way to open conversations
between parent and child.

Opening Moments

Welcome the group and pray this
prayer or one of your own:

> God of all creation and giver of all
> that we need, here we are again,
> eager to become better stewards of
> your creation. Send your Spirit to be
> with us. In Jesus' name, we pray.
> Amen.

Invite participants to tell about
their experiences with acts of giving
and serving since the previous session. If the group is larger than fif-
teen, have them report in groups of

three rather than to the entire group. Allow time for any comments or questions on chapter 3 before moving ahead.

Present the focus question for this session and your plans for it.

For groups of families

Match up families with children of similar ages to report to each other on their acts of giving and serving.

For a retreat setting

Since there will not be enough time to participate in acts of giving and serving, move to questions and comments that have arisen since the previous plenary time.

Personal Experience of the Focus

Materials: paper, pencils

Distribute paper and a pencil to each participant. Give the group three minutes to list five to ten things they would take from their home if they had to leave immediately. (It's understood that no family member is in danger.) When time is up, ask for volunteers to read their lists. Be clear that there is no right answer to the question and that the list is just that: a list quickly made. However, they may want to keep this exercise in mind as they hear the Bible stories.

For groups of families

Materials: paper, pencils, poster board, markers

Invite the families to imagine that they are preparing to move to another country for a year. Much of what they own must be left behind. Invite each family member to decide what five things she or he would take. When they are ready, have each family list the five things for each member on a sheet of poster board. The items can be words or illustrations.

For a retreat setting

Select either activity (Personal Experience or for groups of families) depending on what you know of the group.

Bible Stories

Materials: Bibles

Set the stage for the reading from Exodus by noting that the Hebrews, having escaped Egypt, have been wandering in the desert for about a month now. Read or have a participant read Exodus 16:1–30. Discuss the question on page 38 in chapter 4. Then make the transition to the prayer that Jesus taught his disciples and Luke 11:3 by reading aloud the paragraph introducing Luke 11:3 in chapter 4 (p. 38). Discuss the questions pertaining to Luke 11:3.

For groups of families

Materials: Bible, crackers

Read the Exodus story dramatically and invite the children to moan and complain when you cue them. Distribute crackers to everyone when the manna is gathered. As everyone munches on crackers, move to the discussion of Luke 11:3. While it will not be as exciting as the Exodus story, children who are familiar with the prayer of Jesus will pick up on the conversation.

For a retreat setting

Materials: bread machine, ingredients for bread, Bible, storyteller

Make bread in a bread machine, timing it so it is cooling as you begin this session. Have the storyteller tell the Exodus story. Serve the bread when the manna appears in the story. Go on to discuss Luke 11:3 following the Exodus story.

The Focus and the Bible Stories

Materials: copies of this book, newsprint, markers

Invite the participants to repeat quietly "Give us each day our daily bread" as they look at the lists they created at the beginning of the session. Then ask:

—Which of the items on your list are like daily bread?
—Which provide the sustenance you need daily for growth in body and mind?

Assuming that their lists will include many items that do not provide daily sustenance, introduce the spiritual disciple of fasting, using the

information in chapter 4. Have the group turn to "Seeking a Release from Too Much Stuff," (p. 47). Invite volunteers to read aloud the list of areas to examine. Then ask, "What other areas would you add?" Write their suggestions on newsprint. Finally, have someone read the three steps to fasting. Point out the significance of replacing what is given up with something that brings us closer to God by practicing a spiritual discipline. The spiritual discipline of fasting is not about giving up something or doing without, but a way to help us discover what is most important to us and what is needed for our daily living. It is a way for us to figure out what is "enough" for us.

For groups of families

Materials: copies of this book, posters from the previous activity, markers

Have each family unit gather around its poster. Ask:

—Thinking about the Bible passages, how would you make changes in your list?
—Thinking about Luke 11:3, how would you decide what is necessary for your family to take in addition to the things on your personal lists?

Suggest that they write their answers to the last question on their poster. Bring the families together. Have them name some of the criteria they would use. Move from this discussion to the material on fasting.

For a retreat setting
See the activity for groups of families.

Working with the Focus

Materials: copies of this book

Invite a participant to read the first paragraph of "Decisions about Lifestyle" (p. 40) in chapter 4. Then briefly review the three areas highlighted in chapter 4 and explain why you chose the one you did for their work in this session. Here is a suggested activity for each one:

To a lifestyle that builds community

Materials: copies of this book, drawing paper, pencils, a computer with access to the Internet or printouts from one or more of the Web sites listed in chapter 4

Read "Community Building" (p. 41) in chapter 4. Draw a simple map of your neighborhood. On it write the names of your neighbors on their homes. How many of them do you know? What might you do to get to know more of them, or to get to know some of them better?

To a lifestyle that tends the environment

Materials: copies of this book, writing paper, pencils

Read "Environmental Concerns" (p. 43) in chapter 4. List the ways your family cares for the environment. Make note of ways you want to expand that care. Then discuss the question about "Environmental Concerns" (p. 43).

To a lifestyle that seeks peace

Materials: copies of this book, writing paper, pencils

Read "Working for Peace" (p. 44) in chapter 4. An important way to foster peacemaking is to get to know people who are not like us. Discuss the questions with "Working for Peace" (p. 44). Brainstorm ways to broaden your family's world of friendships.
   Make the following assignments to complete before the next session:
   —Read chapter 4.
   —Follow through on a plan for fasting for your family.
   —Select one of the areas in chapter 4 and begin to work on ways to be good stewards on a daily basis in that area.

For groups of families

Materials: copies of this book, appropriate children's books

Select one activity. Begin by reading a children's book pertinent to that area. See some suggestions in the bibliography for chapter 4. A visit with the children's librarian at your public library will provide other titles. Then talk about the material for that area in chapter 4. Have each family discuss what they might do and select one thing to work on.

For a retreat setting

Materials: copies of this book, a computer with access to the Internet or reprints from one or more of the Web sites listed in chapter 4, drawing paper, writing paper, pencils

Set up activity centers for the three areas in "Working with the Focus," on page 84. Include appropriate children's books in each center. Invite the families to work in each center at their own pace. They might also be encouraged to take a break between centers. Rather than have self-directed centers, consider recruiting a leader for each center who can introduce that topic to each family.

Closing Moments

Materials: copies of this book

Conclude with "A Prayer for Our Stewardship throughout the World" (p. 45). Select someone to read the Leader lines.

Leader Evaluation

What ideas from this session should be given to committees of your congregation? How do you think the participants enlarged their concept of community or stewardship through this session?

The next session concludes this study. Begin to gather resources for participants who want to go further and be prepared to suggest ways for small groups to continue to support one another. What resources from your congregation or community might be helpful to bring to the next session?

Session 5
Just Do It!

Focus Question: Given the ways you now understand your call to be God's stewards, how will you seek justice for all God's creation?

Before You Begin

—Place bookmarks at Amos 5 and Luke 18 in the Bibles.
—Provide additional information about advocacy work in your denomination.
—Cover a wall or a stationary room divider with newsprint for a graffiti wall. (Two layers of newsprint may preserve the wall if the markers bleed through.) Place markers nearby.

Opening Moments

Welcome the participants. Pray this prayer or one of your own:

> God of righteousness, we have found our way here once more. For this final session, we ask that you open our hearts and minds to all people. In Jesus' name. Amen.

Invite any who wish to comment on chapter 4 and their attempts to change their lifestyle or the decisions they made.

Present the focus question and your plan for this session.

For groups of families

Select the way to report information between families that you have found to be most effective in the previous sessions.

For a retreat setting

Move directly to the next activity since there will not be enough time for the group to read chapter 4 or try out lifestyle changes.

Personal Experience of the Focus

Materials: newsprint, markers, masking tape

Point out the graffiti wall you put up earlier. Provide markers (many colors is fun) for the participants to write responses to this question: What is not fair today?

For groups of families

Materials: newsprint, markers, masking tape

Place the graffiti wall on the floor so that family members of all ages can write or draw on it. Have the families first talk about the question, When is something not fair? They can then add their responses together or individually.

For a retreat setting

Materials: newsprint, markers, masking tape

See the activity for groups of families. However, depending on your schedule, you might have the graffiti wall available during free time or a mealtime so that participants can add to it over a longer period.

Bible Stories

Materials: Bibles

Introduce the prophet Amos, with the material in chapter 5 and any other information you have from a study Bible or commentary. Then read Amos 5:14–15 and 21–24. Discuss it, using the question on page 50 of chapter 5.

Then have someone read Luke 18:1–8. Invite the group's comments on the story and discuss the question on page 50 of chapter 5. Read the quote from the elderly minister (p. 50). Ask the group, "What does this say to you about seeking justice?"

For groups of families

Materials: Bibles, persons to portray Amos and the widow

Recruit a man to portray Amos. Introduce him and have him present the verses from Amos 5. He can engage the group in conversation based on the question in chapter 5 (p. 50).

Invite a woman to portray the widow in Jesus' story (Luke 18). Have her tell her story, embellishing the need for justice. Invite both Amos and the widow to talk with the group about justice. Clarify for the children that Amos and Jesus lived centuries apart and that Jesus' story was not about a real widow and judge.

For a retreat setting

Materials: Bibles, storyteller

Present and discuss the stories in Amos and Luke (see the activity for groups of families).

The Focus and the Bible Stories

Materials: graffiti wall, markers, copies of this book

Have the group stand where they can read the comments on the graffiti wall. First, ask them to identify the items on the wall that fit the idea of justice in Amos. Circle those items with a marker. Then select one or two items on the wall. Ask the group, "If this area could be called fair, how would it look?" Then ask, "To change these areas from 'not fair' to 'fair,' what needs to happen?" During this discussion, offer the idea of advocacy, if it does not come from the group. Point out "Be an Advocate" (p. 56) in chapter 5. Invite personal stories about times group members have been advocates for an individual or a group.

For groups of families

Materials: graffiti wall, markers, copies of this book

So everyone is included, ask one or two people to read the items written or illustrated on the graffiti wall. After each one, pose this question: If this situation were made to be fair, how would it look? It is not necessary to discuss each item if some are quite similar. You might, however, want to include any that the children added to the wall.

Then have the group select one notation of an unfair situation from the wall to discuss with this question: To make this situation fair, what has to happen? Then have each family unit select one idea from the wall and create a drawing or "freeze frame" to show it transformed to a scene that is fair. (A *freeze frame* is movement frozen in time.) In the discussion following the presentation of the drawings or freeze frames, bring the group to the idea of advocacy and refer them to "Be an Advocate" (p. 56) in chapter 5.

For a retreat setting

Materials: graffiti wall, copies of this book

Look together at the graffiti wall. Invite the group to look specifically for comments on it that relate to the words from Amos. Then form groups of families of three or four people to create a skit or freeze frame (see the previous activity) of how that unfair idea becomes fair. After each group has presented its skit or freeze frame, ask the group: "What are things you can do to make unfair situations fair?" In the discussion, refer them to "Be an Advocate" (p. 56) in chapter 5.

Working with the Focus

Materials: copies of this book, materials about world and national advocacy groups

Together look at "Advocacy Settings" (p. 50) in chapter 5. Form three workgroups, one each for "congregation," "community," and "world." Give each group any material you gathered or printed from the Internet.

Suggest that each group select one area of concern from those in the chapter or a topic they agree on that fits into that setting. Then brainstorm how they might go about being an advocate in this setting, making use of "Be an Advocate" (p. 56). Each workgroup will report to the other workgroups in a plenary session.

After the work group reports, take a few moments to look at "How to Keep Going" (p. 53) in chapter 5. Invite the participants to take a few moments to think silently about how they will keep up their energy and interest. Encourage them to find partners with whom to follow up this study.

For groups of families

Materials: copies of this book, information about advocacy groups that you have gathered, mural paper, markers, masking tape

In advance, think about each family and determine which area (congregation, community, or world) would best suit them, based on the ages of their children and family interests. For this activity, assign one area to each family. If they wish, two families might work together. (This is sometimes as helpful for parents as it is for the children.) Suggest that they read aloud the appropriate section in chap-

ter 5, select a specific concern in that area, and brainstorm ways to bring justice to that concern. Then together they can create a mural that depicts some of their ideas.

Allow time for everyone to look at the murals. Encourage families with similar interests to work for justice in that area together. Also point out the other ways to keep working for justice in "How to Keep Going" (p. 53) in chapter 5.

For a retreat setting

Materials: copies of this book

Look at the previous activities for this part of the session. Select the one that best fits your group and the time you have as the retreat ends. Whichever choice you make, allow some time for people who are interested in the same area of advocacy to connect. If they wait until they return home, the impetus will be lost.

Closing Moments

Materials: copies of this book

Pray together "A Litany for Seeking God's Justice and Righteousness" (p. 54) in chapter 5.

Read aloud the last paragraph of chapter 5.

Conclude with this benediction:

> Go now in peace, claiming your role as stewards of God's creation. Work for justice and peace, knowing that the Holy Spirit is ever your companion and advocate. Amen.

For groups of families

Materials: copies of this book

Gather any artwork, such as the family posters or mural created earlier, or newsprint lists. Place them in the middle of a large open space and have everyone form a circle around them. Follow the plan under Closing Moments.

For a retreat setting

Materials: copies of this book

Follow the plan under Closing Moments, but intersperse portions of the litanies from the previous sessions as well.

Leader Evaluation

Take time to make notes about your overall impression of this study. Include names of participants as well as what you might change another time. Make general comments as well as comments specific to the use of this guide and book. File them where you will see them when you are ready to plan another similar education event, or give them to the appropriate committee of your congregation.

Notes

Chapter 1: Getting Started

1. Judith E. Smith, "Stewards in the Household of God" in *Weavings, a Journal of the Christian Spiritual Life* 14, no. 5 (September/October 1999): 7. Used with permission.

2. Marjorie J. Thompson, *Family, the Forming Center* (Nashville: Upper Room Books, 1996), 117.

3. The household rules are taken from Judith Smith's article "Stewards in the Household of God" and are based on M. Douglas Meeks, *God the Economist: The Doctrine of God and Political Economy.* (Minneapolis: Fortress, 1989). The questions are from the author.

Chapter 2: At Home

1. Dorothy C. Bass, *Receiving the Day: Christian Practices for Opening the Gift of Time* (San Francisco: Jossey-Bass, 2000), 1.

2. Maria Newman, "Ridgewood Embraces Family Night," *The New York Times,* March 27, 2003, Metro Section, D6. For more information about community family night, see the Web site www.readysetrelax.org.

3. Marjorie J. Thompson, *Soul Feast: An Invitation to the Christian Spiritual Life* (Louisville, Ky.: Westminster John Knox Press, 1995), 129.

Chapter 3: At Church

1. Quoted in *Growing Up Generous: Engaging Youth in Giving and Serving*, by Eugene C. Roehlkepartain, Elanah Dalyah Naftali, and Laura Musegades (Bethesda, Md.: Alban Institute, 2000) from *Developmental Assets: A Synthesis of the Scientific Research on Adolescent Development,* Peter C. Scales and Nancy Leffert (Minneapolis: Search Institute, 1999), 22.
2. Patrick D. Miller, *Deuteronomy*, Interpretation: A Bible Commentary for Teaching and Preaching (Louisville, Ky.: John Knox Press, 1990), 135.
3. Fred Rogers, *The Giving Box: Create a Tradition of Giving with Your Children* (Philadelphia: Running Press, 2000), 87.

Chapter 4: In the Community

1. Neil Douglas-Klotz, *Prayers of the Cosmos: Meditations on the Aramaic Words of Jesus* (New York: Harper & Row, 1990), 26.
2. Kenda Creasy Dean and Ron Foster, *The Godbearing Life*: *The Art of Soul Tending for Youth Ministry* (Nashville: Upper Room Books, 2000), 185.

Chapter 5: Just Do It!

1. Fred B. Craddock, *Luke*, Interpretation: A Bible Commentary for Teaching and Preaching (Louisville, Ky.: John Knox Press, 1990), 210.
2. Kristine A. Haig, "Stewardship: a spiritual practice" in *Presbyterians Today*, November 2001, 4.

Bibliography

Chapter 1: Getting Started

Bass, Dorothy C., ed. *Practicing Our Faith*. San Francisco: Jossey-Bass, 1997. See chapter 8, "Discernment," by Frank Rogers Jr.

Bass, Dorothy C. and Don C. Richter, eds. *Way to Live: Christian Practices for Teens*. Nashville: Upper Room Books, 2002. See the chapter "Choices," by David White with Matthew Mistal.

Jantzi, Jeanne Zimmerly. *Parent Trek*. Scottdale, Penn.: Herald Press, 2001.

Thompson, Marjorie J. *Family, the Forming Center*. Nashville: Upper Room Books, 1996.

Chapter 2: At Home

Bass, Dorothy C. *Receiving the Day*. San Francisco: Jossey-Bass, 2000. Especially chapters 6 and 7.

Caldwell, Elizabeth F. *Making a Home for Faith*. Cleveland, Ohio: United Church Press, 2000. Especially chapters 2 and 5.

Lionni, Leo. *Swimmy*. New York: Alfred A. Knopf, 1963. A story of cooperation and a role for everyone.

Thompson, *Family, Forming Center*, especially chapter 6.

Wehrheim, Carol A. *Children and Money*. Cleveland: United Church of Christ Stewardship Council, 1992. Especially "Allowances: Are They for Your Family?"

Chapter 3: At Church

Brumbeau, Jeff. *The Quiltmaker's Gift*. Duluth, Minn.: Pfeiffer-Hamilton Publishers, 2000. A quiltmaker teaches generosity to a king.

Dean, Kenda Creasy, and Ron Foster. *The Godbearing Life: The Art of Soul Tending for Youth Ministry*. Nashville: Upper Room Books, 1998. Especially chapter 9.

Gomes, Peter J. *The Good Book: Reading the Bible with Mind and Heart*. New York: Avon Books, 1996. Especially chapter 14.

Roehlkepartain, Eugene C., Elanah Dalyah Naftali, and Laura Musegades. *Growing Up Generous: Engaging Youth in Giving and Serving*. Bethesda, Md.: Alban Institute, 2000. Especially chapters 6 and 7.

Rogers, Fred. *The Giving Box: Create a Tradition of Giving with Your Children*. Philadelphia: Running Press, 2000.

Wehrheim, Carol A. *Children and Money*. Cleveland: United Church of Christ Stewardship Council, 1992.

Chapter 4: In the Community

Bass, *Practicing Our Faith*, especially chapter 9. Bass and Richter,

Way to Live, especially the chapters "Creation" (by Frank Rogers Jr. with Timothy Frazier) and "Friends," (by Carol E. Lytch with Katie Lytch).

Coles, Robert. *The Story of Ruby Bridges*. New York: Scholastic, 1995. Ruby's courage and faith are a sign of peacemaking in the midst of hatred and prejudice.

Institute for Peace and Justice at www.ipj-ppj.org. Check out their resources on families and peacemaking.

Vogt, Susan V. *Raising Kids Who Will Make a Difference*. Chicago: Loyola Press, 2002.

Ward, Hiley H. *My Friends' Beliefs: A Young Reader's Guide to World Religions*. New York: Walker and Co., 1988.

Wittman, Sally. *A Special Trade*. San Francisco: Harper & Row, 1978. The friendship between a little girl and an elderly neighbor shows community and friendship at its best.

Wood, Douglas. *Old Turtle*. Duluth, Minn.: Pfeiffer-Hamilton Publishers, 1992. This book sends a message of peace and reminds us that we tend to imagine God as we see ourselves.

Chapter 5: Just Do It!

Bass, *Practicing Our Faith*, especially chapter 4.

Bass and Richter, *Way to Live,* especially the chapter "Justice," by Evelyn L. Parker and Raymond Rivera.

See the following pages for a sample of the companion book to *Giving Together*, also by Carol A. Wehrheim, *Getting It Together: Spiritual Practices for Faith, Family, and Work* (0-664-22582-9).

For more information or to order either of these books, call 1-800-227-2872 or visit our Web site at www.wjkbooks.com.

Getting it Together

Spiritual Practices for Faith,
Family, and Work

Carol A. Wehrheim

Westminster John Knox Press
LOUISVILLE • LONDON

Contents

Introduction

The Williams family, parents Carlos and Jane with their children Maria (8) and Richard (13), live in a midsized city. They are active in their church, attending worship regularly, helping in mission projects, and serving in leadership roles. Both parents are employed full-time, and the children attend nearby public schools.

Three women—Jennie, Martha, and Esther—knew one another previously but became good friends when they attended the same program sponsored by their church on how to live more faithfully. All belong to a large congregation, and all are employed full-time, though Jennie will retire in another year. Martha is the youngest of the three by ten or twelve years. Esther moved to the area a year or so before the church program, while the other two women have lived there most of their lives. They have dinner together at least once a month to talk about their faith and how they are progressing in desired changes in their individual and communal lives.

You will get to know the people described above as you read this book and as they progress through the process suggested here. Like many people, they face the problem of numerous competing claims on their time. Before we learn more about them, however, let's set the stage.

What's the Big Picture?

Before the industrial revolution about two hundred years ago, most families worked side by side, juggling work and family tasks. When men and women began to leave their farm or family business for factories or other places of work, a significant change occurred. In those families where it was possible, the mother stayed home to care for the children and keep house. The men were now the breadwinners, at least for the middle class. This continued to be the desired image, if not always the reality, although the number of working women with school-age children continued to grow.

By 1990, 53 percent of women with preschool children worked, and 66 percent of all mothers worked. For various reasons, from economic need to personal fulfillment, these numbers are not likely to change, and are especially not likely to drop, in the near future. This reality alone might prompt many families to search for ways to balance the personal, work, and church responsibilities they have.

The number of mothers working outside the home is not, however, the only reason that adults today—married and single, parents or not—feel the tension of competing interests and disappearing time. In the 1960s, church leaders talked eagerly of the years ahead when we would all enjoy more leisure time, time to pursue hobbies and intellectual interests as well as to participate in the ministries of our faith communities. Now, near the end of the century, where has that promised leisure time gone?

While technology has provided much to help us in the workplace and at home, it has also increased the pace of our lives. Airmail has given way to e-mail. Answering services and answering machines have become too slow for us, and we have cell phones and pagers so we are never out of reach. A manuscript can be sent to the editor overnight by modem, and the requests for the rewrite are back before you have a chance to take a deep breath. We have little or no "down" time.

For most people, the changes in the workplace add even more pressure. We looked forward to shorter work weeks two or three decades ago, but the average worker in the United States now works significantly more hours than in 1960. If you are not on a career track where a 70-hour week is considered normal, you may be working two or three jobs to pay the bills. Researchers say that many of us suffer from chronic fatigue because, with the increased demands on our time, we sleep too little.

All these factors, along with the stress of life in an age when we know within hours of violence, tragedy, and humanitarian crises in our community and around the globe, put tremendous pressure on adults and children today. We may find ourselves responsible for our parents as well as our children. Whether *you* are in such a bind is not really the issue; for when *others* are, the quality of life for all of us suffers. As Paul wrote to the church in Corinth, "If one member suffers, all suffer together with it" (1 Cor. 12:26).

More Than a Woman's Problem

Articles appear regularly in magazines and newspapers that describe the difficulty of working and raising a family. Usually the articles are directed to women. They may give tips on how to be a "supermom" or say that "you can't have it all." In truth, however, this is not just a woman's problem. People of all ages, genders, career paths, and family situations are caught in the web of competing responsibilities for family, work, and self. For people of faith, these responsibilities, as well as ministry to others, face us daily.

A few conversations with single adults and married couples without children quickly alert you to the stress they are experiencing as well. The grocery store checkout clerk who must care for a parent with Alzheimer's disease is just as affected as the dual-career family trying to find a live-in nanny for their children. The choices we must make daily keep stress high and cause us great anxiety. It doesn't help that many of the causes

of this stress and anxiety are out of our hands.

The Foundation of Our Life

This book is written specifically for Christians and begins with the assumption that, whatever our situation, we must begin by building a firm foundation of faith. The struggle to maintain a balanced life, a life of creative rather than destructive tension, will always be with us. To live with that tension, we are wise if we make time for growing with God our priority. This book is designed to help you make time with God productive through Bible study and specific spiritual disciplines.

Each chapter begins with a selection from Scripture and some words about the passage. You are encouraged to ponder the meaning of the passage for your life today. Take time to read the Bible passage before continuing.

At the conclusion of each chapter is a spiritual discipline. Spiritual disciplines are activities that nurture our spiritual life. While there are many definitions of spirituality today, this book defines it as "the way we choose to live out our faith."[1] Spiritual disciplines or practices help us nurture our faith and grow in our relationship with God. They are essential to a vibrant faith, a faith that will sustain us in this tense, hurried world. Of the many types of spiritual disciplines, five are described in these chapters. Practice each one before you continue to read. Each was chosen to complement that particular chapter.

How to Use This Book

This book consists of five chapters for participants followed by five session guides for a group leader. If you are in a group, your leader will assign the chapters for you to read. If you are not in a group, you might take several weeks to read all five chapters, spacing the reading to give you time to practice some of the suggestions. Try keeping a journal of your experiences and what you are trying. This is particularly helpful if you have no one with whom to discuss your reading, questions, and ideas.

If you are a group leader, be sure to read the participant's chapters as well as the leader's guide for each session.

If you have a spouse or partner, read the book together. Talk about the ideas. Plan ways to try the process. While this is not exactly a how-to book, reading the book without living it is a bit like reading a book on praying but never trying to pray. If you are single or are reading this book on your own, find a friend to discuss it with you. Living faithfully is not something we do alone.